11067248d

ALSO BY PETER BERNHARDT

Wily Violets and Underground Orchids

Natural Affairs

NATURAL AFFAIRS

A Botanist Looks at the Attachments
Between Plants and People

PETER BERNHARDT

Villard Books · New York · 1993

VILLARD BOOKS is a registered trademark of Random House, Inc.

Portions of Chapter 2 appeared in an earlier version in *Garden* magazine,
published by The New York Botanical Garden.
Portions of Chapter 10 appeared in an earlier version in *Good Gardening*
magazine (New Zealand).
Portions of Chapter 13 appeared in an earlier version in *The Sydney Review.*

Library of Congress Cataloging-in-Publication Data

Bernhardt, Peter
Natural affairs: a botanist looks at the attachments between plants and
people/Peter Bernhardt.
p. cm.
Includes bibliographical references and index.
ISBN 0-679-41316-2
1. Plants. 2. Botany. 3. Plants—Folklore. 4. Plants—Social aspects. I. Title.
QK81.B446 1993
580—dc20 92-39149

Manufactured in the United States of America
9 8 7 6 5 4 3 2
First edition

For Jules and Arlene Bernhardt—
two parents who learned to tolerate windowsills crammed with
cacti and ferns, endured insect-filled jars on the summer porch
and a son far too weak in algebra and French skills

Contents

Foreword

When Peter Bernhardt came to the School of Botany at the University of Melbourne in 1978 as a research student, I realized that we had recruited from the United States not only an excellent and careful scientific observer, but one with a genuine fascination for his subject. Like many successful scientific researchers, his approach is imaginative. In the early 1980s Dr. Bernhardt again visited Melbourne Botany, this time to work intensively on a program in pollination biology with Professor Bruce Knox, as part of a team put together in an Australian Centre of Excellence from a grant of the commonwealth government.

Now in 1990/92 he is again back visiting Australia, this time on leave from St. Louis University, Missouri, supported by a *National Geographic* grant and by the Royal Botanic Gardens and Domain Trust in Sydney. The objective of his research is to expose the secret reproductive life of the Australian genus *Hibbertia,* a member of the worldwide family Dilleniaceae (elephant apple or Guinea-flower family), considered by many biologists to possess some of the most primitive features of the flowering plants. Some aspects of the study of Guinea flowers are featured in Chapter 8.

I had other reasons for welcoming Peter back to Australia. Not only was it an opportunity to launch an Australian edition of his very successful earlier book, *Wily Violets and Underground Orchids,* but, more important, it was the opportunity to have working on our staff a scientist who had the ability to communicate to a wide audience the wonders of plants, which is one of the most important roles of a botanical garden.

This book has a different theme from *Wily Violets and Underground Orchids.* Here he looks at ways people relate to plants. To really understand many of the myths that surround plants, we need a scientific explanation. Some folk traditions regarding plants have endured for thousands of years, but rational explanation is a relatively new phenomenon. Plants as folk objects, food, objects of art, of medicine, often have their discovery lost in myth; many today can be explained by science.

Natural Affairs reveals the unfamiliar lives of familiar garden plants, such as magnolias, columbines, and daffodils, as well as the lives of some less familiar plants. The chapters unfold in a personal way, often using artistic and classical allusions to help explain and place into context scientific discovery.

In writing about the plant world, Peter Bernhardt cuts across geographical barriers; ironically, often an exotic plant to an Australian is possibly a common species to a North American. For instance, Californians have adopted our Australian eucalypts, so much so that they sometimes appear to be part of the natural landscape. We in Australia have adopted elms, oaks, and maples, partly in our craving for autumn color. Both of our countries have adopted daffodils *(Narcissus)* as harbingers of spring—strangers to our shores, just as we have both imported *Cannabis,* the source of hemp fiber and of marijuana, products quite unrelated to our spring! Generations of collectors have enriched both public and private gardens with their discoveries.

But it is not only science and scientists on these pages. Peter Bernhardt includes some of the great flower and horticultural writers in the story of plant life. Among them you will find Vita Sackville-West, today probably best known for her great garden at Sissinghurst Castle in Kent, but whose writing on plants is also important. There is also Alice Coats, Edward A. Bowles, and many others.

Not all interpretation of the life of plants is clear sailing. Elements of scientific controversy appear. How could the interpretation of nectaries in plants once have had fascist overtones (Chapter 7)? Why do scientists continue to toy with the reproductive organs of primroses and wood sorrels after 125 years (Chapter 6)? The techniques used to expose the life of plants range from the spade to the electron microscope, from exploring the whole plant to characterizing chemical extracts and molecular details. Some of Dr. Bernhardt's own research has related to plants and animals, especially the insect, bird, and mammal pollinators. In these chapters Peter Bernhardt brings to the reader the enormous progress that is being made in our understanding of the plant world. This understanding reminds us that plants are an essential part of the world we live in.

The image that the study of plants was something to occupy polite ladies in nineteenth-century drawing rooms is an image of botany that is gone forever. Many of the major developments in agriculture, in preservation of the countryside, and in improving life in our urban environments have their roots in botanical sciences. This book gives a lively and scholarly account of the botanist's work. It is sure to inspire those who had not thought about the plant breeders' work on our food. How many of us think, when we eat a tomato, that we are eating a fruit that is in fact a pregnant female, bigger and more flavorsome than nature originally intended? And who would have thought that the green vegetables we so relish, such as lettuce and cabbage, are in fact still virgins!

Dr. Peter Bernhardt demonstrates once again in this book that the science of botany can be most entertaining. The basic factual information has its roots in serious science, and much has been previously published in scholarly journals, some of it from his own researches. This book is more than merely a scholarly scientific account, though. It is a skillful blend of art, literature, science, and scholarship.

Carrick Chambers, Director,
Royal Botanic Gardens, Sydney

PART ONE

The Artist's Vision

CHAPTER 1

Muse Under Glass

The desks were littered with catkins, hazel and willow, which the children had been sketching. But the sky had come over dark, as the end of the afternoon approached: there was scarcely light to draw any more.

D. H. Lawrence, *Women in Love*

Were you born to a royal house or a family of merchant princes? Do you live in a country that experiences hard winters? Do you want your peers to respect your sophistication and be influenced by the fashions set by *your* court?

If you answered yes to all three questions, and lived four to five hundred years ago, you were importing trees and shrubs for your châteaus. Specifically, you imported "tender greens" from the warm, southern lands, especially oleanders *(Nerium oleander)*, pomegranates *(Punica granatum)*, myrtles *(Myrtus communis)*, and lots and lots of citrus. All of these plants would go into large tubs that could be moved about to achieve spectacular effects.

Sour orange *(Citrus aurantium)* and, much later, sweet orange *(C. sinensis)* were the most favored trees. They tolerated severe clipping and made handsome topiaries within the rigid patterns of a formal garden. They also rewarded their owners with the most fragrant blossoms and luxurious fruit of their day. At the first sign of frost, though, their tubs were removed and placed in specially heated buildings until the weather warmed enough to permit them outside. That's why the first greenhouses were called orangeries.

Royal families kept painters to record their wealth and taste, so sprays of orange blossoms and fruiting branches are often depicted in still lifes and in large, specially printed folios (florilegia) that might be regarded as the first "coffee-table books." Sometimes, though, these oranges look rather odd. Their branches seem thin and stringy and they've been twisted into wreaths and garlands. They have a pale, yellowish cast and their leaves are unhealthily small, few and far between. A botanist would say that the branches were etiolated—from the French *étioler*, meaning to become pale and emaciated.

The painters have, in fact, faithfully recorded a tale of desperation. The romantic orangeries were too dark to encourage healthy growth. With insufficient sunlight the orange branches produced hormones known as phytochromes, which allowed new shoots to elongate toward the few, distant sources of light. It was probably the only thing that allowed the trees to survive seasons indoors without a total depletion of their summer reserves.

If you read the old accounts of the head gardeners who maintained the orangeries, you'll note that they were obsessed with keeping the roots of their charges warm instead of ensuring their leaves were well lit. Cold was the implacable enemy, John Gerard concluded after his failure to nurture hibiscus from seed, "notwithstanding one colde night chauncing among many, hath destroied them all." That's why some orangeries were even equipped with shutters, and open fires were often kept burning *inside* the buildings. Although they were later replaced by indoor stoves, such devices spread soot and dried up leaves. The tender greens absorbed more polluted air indoors than out.

Open the windows? You must be joking. Glazing was in its infancy. The few glass panes in the orangeries were small, thick, and could not be opened. Only the south-facing wall was glazed to maximize the penetration of winter sunlight.

Architects, draftsmen, and landscape painters remained faithful to their patrons, leaving us a magnificent record of the transition of the orangery into the greenhouse we know today. Buildings with roofs of transparent glass, complete with ventilation caps, appeared on the great estates through the late 1790s. The technology that gave birth to modern greenhouses had to wait for a real industrial revolution. In the last century, cast iron replaced much stone and brick as the skeleton supporting fine, large panes of thin glass. Such designs spread rapidly from Europe to other parts of the world where gardens froze in winter or dried in summer.

Once Britain repealed its notorious glass tax in 1845, greenhouses became a pleasure even the middle classes could afford. A conservatory attached to a town house (a mansion by our standards) became the fashion in Queen Victoria's day and is with us still. Ironically, the longevity and diversity of greenhouse plants increased only after city skies and rivers grew foul from "progress" and workers sickened in mills and foundries.

Imagine the impact that an ever-expanding selection of public, private, and commercial greenhouses have made on urban artists over less than two centuries. Forced flowers and fruit, while expensive, freed the artist from the rule of the seasons. More important, greenhouses, like zoos, have made the exotic accessible. Bits of South America and Africa could be brought into the dreariest studio without leaving the city. The contents of a public greenhouse or a patron's conservatory filled sketchbooks.

The pavilion of the sleeping princess (she's the cocoon) from *The Loves of Two Insects*, illustrated by J. J. Grandville (1842). European scientists struggled to culture scale insects for cochineal outside Mexico. The pavilion is composed of columns of prickly pear *(Opuntia)*, the insect's food plant, with a roof composed of the pads and flower of a night-blooming cactus *(Epiphyllum)*. Palms and bananas remind you the romance occurs within a Parisian greenhouse.

Frenchman J. J. Grandville (1803–1847) does not seem to have left Paris for the American deserts, yet he drew anatomically precise cacti and succulents while illustrating the silliest fantasies about the passions of these plants and their parasites. Calla lilies and amaryllis will not survive outdoors in The Hague but Piet Mondrian (1872–1944) immortalized them in oils and watercolors and charcoal with his first experiments into modernism around 1910. It's easy to name-drop in the greenhouse and I haven't even mentioned the conservatory canvases of Édouard Manet or the American Impressionist Childe Hassam.

As a botanist, though, what interests me most are the artists whose work shows such intimacy with life under glass that it defines an actual period in their careers. There are two, in particular, who stand out because they were attracted to the same goodies in bloom but interpreted them in opposing ways.

Henri Rousseau (1844–1910) is a naughty pleasure for any botanist or ecologist. Converted into color slides, his pictures are used to introduce the most scientific lectures, although his jungles have less in common with the tropics than a Tarzan movie. Some of Rousseau's friends insisted his leafy landscapes developed from his military memories of Mexico under Maximilian. This tale is treated as fact in some early art books but the evidence now suggests that Rousseau never left France in his life. His tropical studies were inspired by his repeated visits to the greenhouses in the Jardin des Plantes in Paris.

Conversely, some critics insist that the flora of a Rousseau canvas is a complete fantasy—that no such plants exist in nature. Over fifty years ago, Dr. Charles E. Olmstead, at the department of botany of the University of Chicago, took "an expedition" through the Rousseau pictures. While he admitted that most of them were difficult to identify, many plants were still recognizable by their leaves, including the fronds of

In *Repast of the Lion* Henri Rousseau pretends a greenhouse mishmash is an African jungle. To the left is a spiny, New World member of the agave family which prefers arid zones. Lotus blossoms on the right come from warm, Asian waterways. Did the African lion expect Asian bananas for dessert? METROPOLITAN MUSEUM OF ART

palms and cycads, the dragon blood tree *(Dracena)*, and the sharp spears of yuccas. Olmstead also found the foliage of the common snakeplant *(Sansevieria)*, an "immigrant" from warmer climates now sitting on so many windowsills throughout the world.

All of these plants were under glass in public greenhouses before the turn of the century. It's true that Rousseau's vegetation has not been drawn to scale and always lacks anatomical details. Perhaps it was his attempt to "blue pencil" God's mistakes. Like Dr. Olmstead, I see that he's been to the palm, cacti, and succulent houses and all the conservatories with tropical pools.

Since physical size and structure have been left largely to

Rousseau's whims, it does take a little work to identify the flora, but it's not impossible. I once stared at an odd branch in one of his dreamscapes for more than five minutes. I wondered what tropical tree produced hairy, yellow fruits larger than your head and compound leaves like ostrich feathers? *Think small,* an inner voice said, and the mystery tree turned into a sprig of *Acacia* with its yellow flowers compressed into little balls (Chapter 9). Since then I've found the stems of gingers in his work, although he often doesn't care to give them flowers.

One book mentioned that Rousseau collected leaves and grass blades to use as references. It all makes sense, considering the odd proportions within the paintings and how so many scenes seem to consist of curtains of leaves that don't seem to connect to any trunks or vines. When I look at most of these canvases I don't see a landscape with figures. It's more like a still life with figurines. It takes me back to my suburban boyhood when we played with toy soldiers, farm animals, and dinosaurs on the lawn, under the lilac bushes and Japanese maple.

Plant geography isn't Rousseau's strong point either, and species from three continents are combined into what definitely isn't Mexican forest. Let's congratulate the painter for his courage. After all, whole habitats were not a priority of public greenhouses at the turn of the century. Even today, only a few renovated houses take pains to re-create sections of the Amazon basin or assemble exhibits of woody plants standing in rushing waters (rheophytes) from Indonesian rivers. Most tropical houses remain jumbles, not jungles, of specimens that just happen to thrive under similar conditions. Palm or cactus houses are nothing but specialty collections offering living comparisons of plants belonging to the same family but different countries.

From the brush we switch to the camera. From a man whose life touched the beginning of this century we approach an individual whose life missed its end. The work of Robert Mapplethorpe is still so controversial that a discussion of his flower photos suggests I'm playing with notoriety to hold your attention. *Flowers* (Bullfinch Press; Little Brown, 1990), a book of Mapplethorpe's color photos, need not be a source of debate or titillation.

Flowers does suffer from a foreword by Mapplethorpe's friend, Patti Smith, in my opinion. Ms. Smith wants us to believe that Mapplethorpe "came, in time, to embrace the flower as the embodiment of all the contradictions within. Their sleekness, their fullness. Humble narcissus. Passionate zen." She goes on to allude to the "murky heart of a rose" and "the foreskin of a lily."

Why can't the photo of a flower be only the photo of a flower? Jack Walls, one of Mapplethorpe's models, seems to have learned one hard, practical reason why his employer concentrated on flowers, especially toward the end of his life. Interviewed for a documentary, Walls insisted that Mapplethorpe spent more time with flowers *after* he had been diagnosed with AIDS. The photographer seemed to lose his tolerance for people and all the fuss needed to pose celebrities before the lens. "Plants don't talk back," said Walls. "Plants don't blab!" In fact, Mapplethorpe had been photographing tulips, lilies, and some orchids, in black-and-white, since the late seventies. Only the color photographs, published posthumously, can be dated to his final years.

Examining the collection in *Flowers* confirms the notes I've made after viewing random selections of Mapplethorpe's black-and-white photos of plantlife. Over 75 percent of the pictures in the book feature blossoms grown in commercial greenhouses. Many of the "models" were orchids, aroids (the philodendron family), and a bouquet resembling heliconias. All of these plants have a tropical- or Mediterranean-zone history. They also show the obvious marks of selective breeding and hybridization for greenhouse culture.

With some confidence I might also add that the subjects of the vast majority of Mapplethorpe's photos of long-stemmed roses were produced in commercial greenhouses. A regime of pruning up to twice a year, coupled with controlled temperatures and spraying, ensures "leggy buds" that mature at the same time and are devoid of pest-made holes. Greenhouse roses are always available and they permitted Mapplethorpe a lot of photography in the last years of his life.

The fanciest flower dealers in Manhattan seem to have had a good customer in Mapplethorpe. Specimens that could have come out of a suburban garden are almost impossible to find in his work. Like Rousseau, Mapplethorpe appreciated his subjects but made no attempt to find out what they were. Two photos in the book are entitled Jack-in-the-Pulpit. In fact, they are of the hollow, vaselike leaves of pitcher plants *(Sarracenia)*. Pitcher plants are "meat eaters" digesting the insects that tumble down their vases and drown in their hidden puddles. While they are common enough in the swampier regions of the eastern half of the United States, it's illegal to pick them. Those appearing in the most expensive flower arrangements are grown under glass by nurserymen faithfully re-creating the conditions of quaking bogs and sphagnum moss mats.

Mapplethorpe was pleased with his results and said his photos were "not sweet. They are New York flowers. Nobody else can photograph flowers the way I do. They have a funny kind of black edge to them, I think." Maybe so, but orchids and aroids still carry special features that have not been lost by glasshouse pampering. Such reproductive organs were "preadapted" for Mapplethorpe's studio, since they had to survive under the hot lights. A blossom that lives for a week or two in the wild is ideal for a fussy photographer posing, re-posing, and then disposing of wilted models. The green patterns in some orchid petals and in the hoods and funnels (spathes) of some of the aroids suggest they contain reasonable levels of chlorophyll that fed the blossom long after it had been severed from its leafy stem.

Orchids and aroids must often wait a long time for cross-pollination in nature, as most tropical species make no nectar or offer much edible pollen. Some species secrete oily fragrances gathered by bees completing a complex stage in their life cycles (Chapter 10). Cologne collection is not the only priority in the bee's life, so the flower must last until the moment is right. Other orchids and aroids offer no reward at all. Mapplethorpe actually photographed living traps that may entice bees, gnats, or dung beetles into the blossom with color and scent cues then hold them prisoner until the plant receives or releases pollen. An enduring, strong trap must be reinforced. Mapplethorpe's subjects contain tough veins and fibers. More important, these organs are covered with a thick, fatty cuticle serving as a combination sunblock and lid to restrict water vapor from escaping succulent tissues. That's what gives so many of the flowers in his black-and-white photos a waxy look, as if they were melting candles. It's not a camera trick.

Mapplethorpe's preoccupation with the Asian slipper orchids known as paphiopedilums is particularly engrossing once you know the full story. *Paphiopedilum* (Greek for Venus's sandal) consists of about forty species distributed from the Himalayas through the forests of New Guinea. They are very closely related to the moccasin flowers and lady's slippers *(Cypripedium)* of North America but paphs are far easier to grow and have been greenhouse plants since the last century. Paphiopedilums have their own black edge. The lateral petals and a central, shieldlike organ known as the staminode are often ornamented with hairy warts. Mapplethorpe's camera caught the glistening lumps on the petals in all their winking glory. No one really knew if these sculptures had any real function. In the greenhouse, such orchids were depen-

Slipper Orchid by Robert Mapplethorpe (1987). Has the photographer given this flower a black edge, *or* does lighting merely emphasize a few recurrent "tricks" of tropical evolution? Note the "hairy warts" on the drooping lateral petals and the honeycomb pattern decorating the shield-like staminode in the center.

dent on man for pollination and a long program or commercial hybrids had been the result.

That was until Dr. John Atwood, of the Marie Selby Gardens in Florida, visited populations of *P. rothschildianum* in
eastern Malaysia, publishing his results in 1985 (it's unlikely
Mapplethorpe read the paper). Hairy warts appear to mimic
the bodies of aphids and other sucking bugs that are preyed
upon by female hover flies *(Dideopsis aegrota)*. Under normal
circumstances the fly lays an egg on a luckless aphid and the
hatching maggot devours its host. A pregnant fly visiting the
paph flower mistakes the warts on the staminode for real
bugs. In her attempt to lay eggs she falls off the slippery
surface into the bucket-shaped lip petal. When she crawls out,
though, her escape route must take her under the pollen-
receptive tip of the pistil and then under the organs shedding
sticky pollen. The fly that repeats her errors on two different
plants has cross-pollinated one of the orchids. Fly eggs laid on
the orchid hatch and die without appropriate food while the
flower develops hundreds of good seeds. Deceiving expectant
mothers and starving their babies seems far more perverse
than any of the antics of the leather men Mapplethorpe
photographed. I wonder how Senator Jesse Helms missed
that bit?

There is no Muse of botany or horticulture. Urania helped
astronomers but paid no attention to the life sciences. Nevertheless, plants inspire all the arts without the aid of any of the
nine daughters of Zeus. Some artists have preferred to stay
indoors for almost five hundred years to find plants worthy of
their attention. As forests shrink even further those artists will
be treated less as eccentrics and more as front-runners in a
torch race.

CHAPTER 2

....

A Sanctuary
for the Dreamtime

And this our life, exempt from public haunt,
Finds tongues in trees, books in the running brooks,
Sermons in stones, and good in every thing . . .

William Shakespeare, *As You Like It*

The Dandenong Ranges, less than an hour's drive east of Melbourne, Australia, are well loved but rather low. The highest point, on Mt. Dandenong, is only about nineteen hundred feet above sea level. On weekends and holidays these ranges are filled with urban visitors who come to browse in the local galleries, explore the bulb and shrub nurseries, or follow a relaxing drive in the country with a Devonshire-style tea (steaming teapots are accompanied by freshly baked scones served with berry jams and thickened cream). Almost everyone visits Sherbrooke State Forest, as patient naturalists seek glimpses of rare plants and songbirds.

One place in the Dandenongs, the William Ricketts Sanctuary, defies an easy classification. Is it best regarded as a small forest preserve or a sculpture garden? Should we approach it as a shrine, as it is meant to be a tribute to the beliefs of the Australian aborigines? Billy Ricketts, the creator of the sanctuary that bears his name, is of European descent. He was born in the Melbourne suburb of Richmond in 1906. Now in his late eighties, he originally wanted to be a musician. "I tried to play the violin," he told me back in 1983. "It was a genuine mistake." He played violin in theater orchestras for silent films. "Talkies" forced him to search for a new trade. Billy went to live in central Australia in the early 1930s. He camped among the Pitjantjatjara people and was deeply touched by the remnants of their hunter-gatherer culture in the desert. Despite never having had training in the arts, Billy started sculpting to help interpret his impressions of the aborigines' stories of creation. Some of these early works are still displayed at a tourist attraction just outside the town of Alice Springs.

The severe encroachment of white society and its subsequent mistreatment of the aborigines distressed him. For these and other reasons he developed a reputation around Alice Springs as a "ratbag" (a crank). Old-timers still laugh at the memory of Billy wandering around the arid scrub "mending" holes in his sweaters with bits of twigs and thorns.

Around 1934 he arrived in the Dandenongs where he had earlier bought about five acres of land. He supported himself by selling those of his figurines he found imperfect. "The white man's business had driven me here," he said. Billy never married. His mother kept house for him for decades, although "house" was little more than a sheet-metal shack.

He recalled that when he first started living in these mountains, the Dandenongs were on fire. "Loggers had been here. They came in to wreck it." Billy decided to plant nothing, but to let the forest regenerate. "I'm here to love it," he said. "Trees know more than the Forests Commission."

Billy began to sculpt on his land. The property was transformed by a combination of fired-clay figures and friezes along with the ongoing process of regrowth. The unique quality of the sanctuary is based on the way the art and habitat merge and transcend. Journalists who visited Billy in the fifties and sixties often referred to him as a crusader or evangelist in clay. The sculptures Billy made are infused with his own concepts of spirituality, but also reflect his determination to capture the essence of aboriginal religion. Myths often vary a lot between tribes, but most aboriginal groups believe that the earth and sky have always existed. During the "dreamtime," spirit ancestors rose from beneath the earth to bring light and form to the world. After filling Australia with its plants and animals, these beings quarreled with one another and became afflicted with weariness. Some sank back into the rocks or changed into trees, celestial bodies, or geological formations.

The sanctuary pieces reflect this mythos. Archetypal adult figures merge with the boulders and appear to be sinking into the rock. Beards turn green with algae and blend with trickling water. Their legs become roots or end in reptilian claws. Most aboriginals believed that spirits made babies and then hid them in rocks and trees until a prospective mother walked by. Billy has interpreted this by having the beguiling faces of children seem to jump out of the stones lining sanctuary pathways.

Not all the figures are of aborigines. One motif that recurs is of a strong white man, often with a lyrebird *(Menura novaehollandiae)* perched on his shoulder. Billy used himself as the model for this figure but it represents *his* belief that the European can become part of the Australian environment if he is willing to learn from the aborigines. Billy remembered one resident, a female lyrebird: "Mother nested here every year. She brought them [her fledglings] into the house. I gave them a spot of cheese occasionally. It was wrong, but what can you do?"

Billy learned to achieve the effects he wanted by using some of the natural ingredients on his property. Red clay came from a deposit in the land. Figures were molded directly onto the rock, then removed and fired in a homemade brick oven

Billy poses by a frieze of European man with his lyrebird totem. Man and artwork are framed by the fronds of native tree ferns. PHOTO BY JOHN KELLY

fed by coal, coke, or oil (this was replaced by an electric kiln in the sixties). When the piece came out of the kiln it was fixed to its rock with steel pins.

Impervious to the damp weather, the sculptures have a glassy texture although they have never been glazed. Bathed by the drip and mist of fountains (developed by diverting a natural spring) and the deep shade of the forest canopy, the very surface of the artwork has been colonized by crustose lichens, blue-green algae (cyanobacteria), leafy liverworts, and pigeon moss *(Polytrichum)*. Seams between boulders and their sculpture borders have filled with the small but intricate growth of maidenhair ferns *(Adiantum)* and ivy-leaf violet *(Viola hederacea)*. As the sculptures continue to provide refuge for germinating spores and seeds, even the humblest organisms can take the hard edge off the figures, giving them a feeling of timelessness.

The faces of aboriginal children are colonized by the vegetative, "leafy" phase in the life cycle of local mosses. PHOTO BY JOHN KELLY

Professor of anthropology T. G. H. Strehlow recognized this effect when he wrote of Billy's work (in a booklet published by the Forests Commission):

> His best group sculptures are admirably fitted together: they are devoid of superfluous lines and contradictory motifs. What could have remained a dead background in the works of men of lesser skill here becomes an integral and living part of the whole: for the clay base from which the figures spring and across which these liquid lines flow suggests a live, plastic earth still giving birth to totemic personages, and their plants and animals.

The sanctuary is now enveloped by the dynamic regrowth of hard-leaf (sclerophyll) trees growing in a relatively rich volcanic loam. Australian ecologists would classify the structure of the vegetation as tall open forest and tall woodland with an alliance of eucalypts favoring mountain ash *(Eucalyptus reg-nans)* and manna gum *(E. viminalis)*. The grayish-green sheen and brick tones of the sculptures are broken by the broadly erect, white trunks of these trees. This effect is never monotonous or gloomy. Additional colors are provided in late spring and early summer by the yellow pom-poms of two *Acacia* species and the purplish-blue flowers of mintbush *(Prostanthera lasianthos)*.

The Dandenongs are small but they are a natural catch-ment area and their gullies have provided a refuge for unusual plants as the continent has dried. In my opinion, it's the sanctuary's population of wild fern trees that gives Billy's work its distinctive presentation. Soft tree ferns *(Dicksonia antarctica)* and rough tree ferns *(Cyathea australis)* can grow up to twenty feet high. Their wheels of huge fronds are the perfect foil for sanctuary figures. As the angle of sunlight changes during the day, their feathery shadows dapple sculpted faces, breasts, and limbs.

Billy's friends and admirers convinced him to sell his land to the Forests Commission of Victoria, which promised to preserve the land and let him continue to live on the site. In the early sixties the Forests Commission expanded the sanc-tuary to almost twelve acres, replaced Billy's studio, and built him a more comfortable house a few feet from the old shack. The sanctuary was opened to the public in 1964, and there is still a small charge for admission to fund perpetual mainte-nance.

This has not answered all of Billy's concerns. With so much public use the Dandenongs could never remain pristine. The degradation of the habitat by introduced plants may be seen throughout much of the mountain range. As the Dan-denongs have grown more suburbanized, both garden plants and weeds from Europe, South America, and South Africa have become entrenched in the absence of their natural enemies. One need only cross the road in front of Ricketts's sanctuary to find flourishing blankets of wandering jew *(Tradescantia fluminensis)*.

Alien plants continue to invade the sanctuary. I found parrot flowers *(Alstroemaria)* from South America and hydrangeas from Asia gaining footholds. The greatest threat, though, is European ivy *(Hedera helix)*. It creeps up over the statues and trunks of the fern trees. The increasing weight of the ivy vines can pull the fern trees down, and once the vines smother the fern tree's single growing shoot and cover the fronds, the victim starves for lack of light. A sarcastic remark attributed to Frank Lloyd Wright is applicable here: "Doctors bury their mistakes. Architects plant ivy." Let's hope the Forests Commission keeps such invaders under control. The work is endless, as birds eat ivy berries and defecate the seeds intact. Reinfection of the sanctuary is a cyclical process.

Lyrebirds were once common throughout the Dandenongs. Overdevelopment on Billy's side of the mountains has destroyed much of their habitat, and their totemic spirit survives now only in clay on sanctuary grounds. "Cats and dogs have ripped through everything," Billy complained. Vandals have also inflicted damage, and some sculptures have missing portions. Billy displayed surprisingly little animosity toward such people. "They pay a visit in periods a few years apart." He has not "had time" to attend to repairs.

Billy has great hostility for the Forests Commission, which has in fact been most generous with him. He refuses to believe the commission actually owns the property. "They don't own it. It belongs to people of the whole universe including worms in the earth." In contrast to Billy's hostility to the commission is his entirely positive attitude toward tourists. "Only ten percent are just sightseers," he affirms. "People come in with love and respect and they come out more embellished."

Indeed, judging by the guest book one signs before leaving,

the public is enthusiastic and appreciative. Its effect on first-time visitors is startling. Academic-author George Seddon noticed that visitors "talk in whispers as if they were in church." Viewers from India seem particularly impressed, and certainly the multiple heads, arms, and flowing beards offer a parallel with Hindu sculpture.

As for me, I couldn't help being reminded of the illustrations of William Blake, especially in the larger pieces. Surely there is a touch of *Job* in these craggy faces? I asked Billy if he had taken inspiration from Blake's work, and he laughed. It seems that years ago, when he first settled in the Dandenongs, a local newspaperman referred to him as a "William Blake of the latter day."

"I know nothing of Blake," he said with a tolerant smile.

PART TWO

Tasteful Botany in Three Courses

CHAPTER 3

....

Seven Families
in One Salad

I never had a specially intimate contact with botany. In
my preliminary examination in botany I was also given
a Crucifer to identify—and failed to do so. . . . It oc-
curred to me that artichokes were Compositae, and indeed I might fairly have called them my *favourite flowers.*
Being more generous than I am, my wife often brought
me back these favourite flowers of mine from the market.

Sigmund Freud, *The Interpretation of Dreams*

By the time we returned from the mall, neither my
wife nor I wanted whatever we had defrosted for dinner. Salad
and cold meat would make a good substitute. I had already
spent the early morning shopping at the Soulard Market.
Established since the 1840s, it's one of the oldest surviving
farmers' markets west of the Mississippi River and worth a visit
if you're in St. Louis. The produce on sale changes with the
season, ethnic makeup, and the traditions of an urban working class whose families arrived as rural poor.

I've included a list of what we ate in one bowl, but don't
expect an apology if our tastes conflict. Unlike Nora Ephron,
for example, I don't believe "that any dish that tastes good
with capers tastes even better with capers not in it." Since

Peter Bernhardt

Table 1. Salad Components from a Saturday Dinner

Name	Origin or Region of Earliest Cultivation	Family	Edible Organ(s)	Eaten When Mature?
artichoke *(Cynara scolymus)*	Mediterranean	Compositae (thistle-daisy)	flowering head	no
capers *(Capparis spinosa)*	Mediterranean	Capparidaceae (clammy weeds)	flower bud	no
celery *(Apium graveolens* var. *dulce)*	Europe/Italy	Apiaceae (carrot-dill)	leaf stalk (petiole)	yes
cucumber *(Cucumis sativus)*	India	Cucurbitaceae (gourd-melon)	fruit (ovary)	no
lettuce *(Lactuca sativa* var. *romana)*	Mediterranean	Compositae (thistle-daisy)	leaf blade (lamina)	yes
radish *(Raphanus sativus)*	Asia Minor	Cruciferae (cabbage-cress)	taproot	yes
scallion *(Allium caepa)*	Turkestan	Liliaceae (tulip-lily)	bulb, leaves (stem shoot)	yes
tomato *(Lycopersicon esculentum)*	Peru	Solanaceae (nightshades)	fruit (ovary)	yes

capers are pickled in salty vinegar and artichoke hearts are steeped in oil, combining the two with fresh vegetables means you don't have to think about adding extra salad dressing.

Even overeducated people insist they have little intimate contact with botany, although it remains one of the few sciences we put in our mouths every day. The process of buying and preparing food turns most kitchen counters into botanical gardens in miniature. The salad bowl tells an old story in which different civilizations have tackled the same problems in the geography, classification, anatomy, and development of plants. If we investigated this salad, we would start looking at maps but end up peering through the microscope.

Locating the true region of origin or the earliest evidence of cultivation for a single vegetable is among the most difficult tasks for a scientist. Most of the plants in my salad have been cultivated for so long that mankind transported them from country to country long before written records existed or long after such records crumbled to dust. Celery is one of the few exceptions. Its immediate ancestors continue to grow as marsh plants throughout much of Europe. The Italians appear to have been the first to have grown tired of risking wet feet and snakebite every time they wanted crispy stalks. By the seventeenth century the French had picked up celery culture from the Italians, but it was unknown through most of Britain until well into the Victorian period.

In contrast, although certain plants are automatically associated with the "flavor" of a particular country, we must be reminded that their association with some cuisines has often been rather brief. The tomato sauces in your favorite Italian restaurant or pizzeria were part of the wealth of Mexico taken by Spanish conquistadores or their churchmen. They plucked the tomato from Aztec gardens, but it now looks as if the Aztecs received their vines via Peru during a course of overlapping pre-Columbian trade over thousands of years. That's why tomato breeders, attempting to develop disease-resistant strains, must gather "wild genes" surviving in the Andes.

The geographical pattern in this salad bowl does have a recurrent theme, in that many species originated or were first cultivated around the Mediterranean Sea or in the adjacent lands of Asia Minor. I don't think this reflects the bias of Soulard shoppers or a tasteful coincidence on my part. Yes, my salad could have had a sharper, tropical American slant had a ripe avocado *(Persea americana)* or bell pepper *(Capsicum annuum)* been available that morning. However, avocado and bell pepper were also treasured upon their introduction to the Mediterranean. Today, Israel is one of the world's leading exporters of avocados, and sweet peppers remain a treasured component of antipasto plates. The Mediterranean remains an irresistible "magnet" attracting edible plants from the obscurest regions.

The Mediterranean gave Western civilization its salads. Here we find the earliest written records of boiled vegetables allowed to cool off in a piquant marinade or just cut up raw and eaten in oil and aromatic herbs. The Mediterranean connection may be reflected in the common or scientific names of some species. The word *scallion* is a corruption of *Ascalon,* a biblical port. *Artichoke* is a word of Arabic origin but the plant belongs to the genus *Cynara,* which may refer to an Aegean island esteemed by Imperial Rome as the "home of the artichoke."

Outside the Mediterranean, salads have remained an "acquired" taste subject to sporadic bursts of popularity, especially in British and Germanic cultures. Someone always seems to be rediscovering "humane and healthful eating habits" in colder climates, but the fortunes of salad eaters and salad makers have been variable outside the Mediterranean basin. After all, don't folktales like "Rapunzel" or "Parsley Girl" warn expectant mothers about accepting leafy greens from strange women? Brillat-Savarin wrote that fashionable

London went through a salad craze in the early 1800s. An exiled Frenchman made his fortune going from house to house preparing salads for dandies and their ladies. This salad caterer grew so prosperous he had a special mahogany case made to carry a range of vinegars, flavored oils, anchovies, truffles, and even raw egg yolks so he could literally whip up mayonnaise on demand.

Obviously, this fad didn't last, as Englishmen and their descendents have tended to be more restrained in their praise of salad, often finding something miserly and eccentric in a countryman who forces his friends to dine on raw vegetables. You could see their point if you ordered a salad in most traditional Australian restaurants less than a decade ago. A plate would arrive containing a leaf of lettuce, a wedge of tomato, an onion ring, a slice of canned beetroot, and half a hard-boiled egg!

In contrast, salads are such an enduring part of Mediterranean culture that their uses have ranged from the sacred to the satirical. For example, ancient Egyptians believed the souls of their dead hungered for the foods they enjoyed in life, so cucumbers were entombed with the pharaohs, even though this vegetable seems to have originated in India. Their priests insisted that a salad once made a male deity pregnant! Isis, the Great Enchantress, punished her brother, Set, after he attempted to rape her son, Horus. Set controlled the scorching winds, but he ruled over only wastelands and regarded lettuce as a rare treat. Isis never told her brother that she dressed his salad with a potion made with the semen of Horus. Set suffered such a cosmic case of morning sickness that he vomited up the eye of the sun, Ra-Harakhte. When Set "gave birth," Thoth, the god of scribes, emerged from his head.

Pesach, or Passover, remains my favorite holiday. A ceremony (the seder) commemorating the miraculous escape of the Jews from Egyptian bondage is held at the dinner table on the first two nights of the holiday. Different foods and wine are combined to re-create aspects of The Book of Exodus. The first solid food taken during the seder is raw, leafy greens (parsley, watercress, or lettuce will do) dipped in a little salt water. The greens are usually seen as a token of gratitude to God for all the good things grown by the earth, but salt water represents tears. As a child, I was taught that since Passover comes in the spring we are recalling the tears shed in slavery when we taste the green herbs of the season.

On a more humorous note, we have salad jokes in the plays of Aristophanes. In *The Peace,* the War Spirit attempts to turn the bickering city-states into the ultimate Greek salad, with each city representing a different vegetable, cheese, or seasoning. In *The Birds,* the hoopoe king tells two disaffected Athenians that his feathered subjects enjoy a pleasant diet that sounds a lot like a combination of greens and the sort of seeds baked into ancient wedding cakes. Here is a translation provided by Benjamin Bickley Rogers:

Hoopoe: Then in the gardens we enjoy the myrtles, the cress, the poppy, the white sesame.
Euelpides: Why, then ye live a bridegroom's jolly life.

Of course, the Roman emperor Augustus would never have believed such a fanciful tale. "A radish may know no Greek, but I do" was his sarcastic expression when warning potential deceivers that he was nobody's fool. Even so, the emperor's banquets began or ended with raw lettuce, as Romans believed it relaxed their bowels: "*Prima tibi dabitur ventri Lactuca movendo Utilis*" (Source: Martial, *Epigrams*). But more on this later (p. 34).

It's the radish, though, that allows us to exchange salad geography for the classification of salad species. Radishes are crucifers and belong to the same plant family Sigmund Freud failed to identify as a student. This means that red radishes

(Raphanus sativus) are intimately linked with other vegetables like horseradish *(Armoracia rusticana)* and cabbage *(Brassica oleracea* var. *capitata).* In fact, red radishes and cabbages are so closely allied that they may be hybridized artificially even though the fertile offspring is of no commercial value. Radishes also share the same family tree as over three thousand other species of crucifers (although most are inedible). This includes woad *(Isatis tinctoria),* the source of a blue dye that once stained the skins of orthodox druids, and such old-fashioned flowers as the alyssums *(Alyssum* spp.), wallflower *(Cheiranthus cheiri),* and honesty or moneyplant *(Lunaria rediviva).*

While the species in this salad share distributions, their respective classifications give some indication of the vast diversity of flowering plants. Only two plants in the bowl, artichoke and lettuce, can be placed in the same family.

Frenchman Pierre Magnol (1638–1715) is generally credited as being the first taxonomist to organize the myriad plant species into families based on shared likenesses. This pigeonholing made it much easier to identify plants in books. You could look up a chapter in which all the species had overlapping features instead of reading through hundreds of pages of unrelated descriptions in the hope of stumbling across the proper match.

Today, of course, organization within any family of plants, animals, or even microbes should indicate a real family tree with branches designating a common evolutionary origin. Botanists link plant species together in the same family in much the same way that zoologists link together animal species. The features of the skeletons, guts, egg shape, nest architecture, etc., place the domestic pigeon, turtledove, and even the extinct dodo in the family Columbidae. The architecture and arrangement of stems and leaves, construction of flowering heads, and the number of floral organs and seeds place lettuce and artichoke in the Compositae. Of course, shared characters must be continually tested and expanded. Pollen grain and embryo structure, chromosome number and cell chemistry are just a few of the features modern botanists consider when they revise a plant family.

It's still possible to identify most plants down to family by dissecting their flowers, counting the organs in each organ ring, and noting how those organs attach to each other. The result will give you a little formula of identification for the family. For example, a radish flower would give you this simple formula:

$$K \quad 4 \quad C \quad 4 \quad A \quad 6 \quad (2 \ + \ 4) \quad G \quad \textcircled{2}$$

Written out, this would mean that the calyx (K) consists of four separate sepals. The corolla (C) is made of four separate petals. The androecium (A) consists of two rings of pollen-making stamens with two in the outer ring and four in the inner ring. The gynoecium (G) consists of a single, seed-making pistil, in which two smaller pistils have united together forming one compound organ. Now compare the radish formula to the formula for an artichoke or lettuce flower:

$$\overline{K \quad i \quad C \quad \underline{5} \quad A \quad \overline{5} \quad G \quad \textcircled{2}}$$

The calyx (K) consists of an indeterminant (i) number of little sepals reduced to scales or threadlike tufts. The corolla (C) consists of a tube of five petals all united together at a common base. The androecium (A) is made of five stamens in a single ring but the tips of the stamens interconnect forming a hollow tube around the neck of the gynoecium (G) that is made of two united pistils. The bottom line linking all four rings means that the seed box of the gynoecium is the lowest structure in the flower and all the other flower parts are ultimately attached to it.

Like many extended clans, the members of some plant families are cherished by us, while we look upon certain "cousins" with mistrust. Would you refuse a fresh tomato even though it belongs in the family of nightshades? When some of the tomato's cousins are eaten they may cause delirium and hallucinations, glaucoma, a trancelike state, or death. Some nightshade chemicals, like nicotine, are deadly because they are so addictive in small quantities. Others, like hyoscyamine, are fatal to adults even if taken in a few tiny berries. How can we feel so secure when we slice a tomato into a bowl?

The easiest way to answer that question is to shift from classification to anatomy. Plants employ a battery of toxins to discourage foragers. The tomato is no exception and contains the sickening compounds tomatine and tomatidine in its stems and leaves. The ripe fruit is another matter, though. Most fleshy fruits advertising glossy colors when ripe and containing many small seeds employ a wide range of animals to act as their agents of seed dispersal. It would not do at all if the flesh of the tomato harmed or killed the bird, monkey, or tortoise in the act of ferrying tomato seeds through its guts. So, serious poisons are restricted to those of the vine's organs which provide support (the stems) and convert water and carbon dioxide into food (the leaves).

That's one reason why the salad bowl is such a Frankenstein's monster of parts. Few plants are eaten in their entirety, although organs are not always rejected because they're poisonous. They may be too tough to chew, too bitter, or just tasteless. The scallion was the only component in my salad bowl that offered more than one edible organ, but this reflects a simple matter of continuity. The white "bulb" of a scallion is not a root at all. You cut off the bearded bundle of true roots when you clean the scallion. No, the white bulb is really a succulent, underground stem and the plumpness of each bulb depends on the white, fleshy "leaves" that form the storage layers surrounding the growing tip hidden in the center of the bulb. In scallions the innermost layers of the bulb grade continuously into long, tender, green, hollow leaves that poke well above the soil surface. You may chop most of these green leaves into the bowl and discard their weathered, wilting tips.

Our eating habits have become so specific, though, that we prevent certain parts of the same organ from entering a salad bowl. Most of the leaves of the majority of flowering plants consist of two interconnecting parts. There is a leaf stalk, known as the petiole, that anchors the leaf to the stem. The petiole "ends" in a flattened, expanded surface that does most of the work of photosynthesis and sends the sugars it makes back into the stem or down to the roots for storage. This flattened structure is called the blade.

Celery and lettuce are eaten for their leaves, but salads contain the petioles of the celery and the blades of the lettuce, not vice versa. The petioles of lettuce leaves are far too short and tough to merit attention. The blades of a celery leaf subdivide into lots of little bitter leaflets.

Harvesting a crop at its "peak of ripeness" is a bit of advertising hype that means very little when you compare the plant organs of eight species in seven plant families with very different habits of development. Four species are eaten only for their vegetative organs and they must be picked before the plant shows any sign of sexual maturity. Yes, *every* supermarket lettuce dies a virgin.

Allow a lettuce in a garden bed to produce its cute little head of yellow flowers and you might as well plow it under. It has become far too fibrous, but, more important, it exudes a bitter milky fluid when cut. The earliest civilizations around the Mediterranean must have known lettuce as a bitter herb. Modern breeding has been able to suppress the production of latex until the lettuce begins to flower and specialized cell clusters (lactifers) are activated in lower stems and leaves. The edible lettuce *(L. sativa)* has a close relative *(L. virosa)* that was *never* destined for dinner. People thought that the latex in this bitter lettuce was akin to the white milk in an opium poppy, so its juice was taken medicinally as a cough suppressant, diuretic, and early tranquilizer!

Of the four reproductive organs that went into the salad, only one was eaten at "functional maturity." Stopping development to preserve peaks in flavor and digestibility becomes much more obvious if we lay those organs end-to-end, with the oldest stage always following the youngest. The artichoke "heart" is really a very young phase in the life of a flowering head (involucrum) that would resemble a blooming thistle if spared the pruning hook. To preserve the succulence but increase tenderness, the prickly, protective leaf scales were stripped away. The young head, consisting of hundreds of flower buds, was quartered, cooked, then preserved in oil.

The caper has been taken only one step further. We've waited until naked flower buds emerged from the young, flowering stalk. Picked buds are allowed to wilt and are then fixed in brine and vinegar. The bottled caper bud will never be allowed to open its petals and thrust its many sexual organs into the sunlight.

At first, the cucumber looks like it has been allowed to go all the way. Sperm reached the pistil's ovary fertilizing a new generation of seeds. The receptive tip and neck of the pistil dried up and dropped off, but the ovary swelled to such large, durable dimensions it could be transported fresh. But . . . is the cucumber a fruit that is eaten ripe? Not when you compare it to its cousins in the gourd and melon family. Cucumber skin (exocarp) is still green when peeled, so it has not been allowed to go through the yellowing and mottling of maturity. The middle layer of flesh (mesocarp) contains tissues that are still firm instead of the soft, squashy combination of placental strings and oozing walls associated, say, with the interior of a mature pumpkin *(Cucurbita pepo)* or cantealoupe *(C. melo)*. The cucumber's seeds have not been given time to harden their coats. Cucumber development must be arrested because it does not keep its blandness at maturity. Its interior turns into a fibrous slush and the fruit's husk expels its seeds gloppily when pressure is applied. Within the Cucurbitaceae, the cucumber belongs to a tribe that fills its fruits with bitter-tasting substances (cucurbitacins) as its seeds grow shells and its skin changes color. When such noxious fruits are consumed they can be a source of violent cramps. Wild relatives have caused the death of horses.

The preoccupation with the perfectly developed, perfectly prepared cucumber seems "very British," but it predates teatime traditions by more than seventeen hundred years. When Roman doctors placed Emperor Tiberius on a cucumber diet in the first century A.D., the imperial gardeners were faced with the problem of inducing a warm-weather vine to fruit in winter. They devised the West's first hothouse, growing the plants under protective, transparent slabs of a sheet rock known as mica.

Not everyone sharing the English language has agreed that the fruit pleases all English tongues. Samuel Johnson was a cucumber curmudgeon who said, "A cucumber should be well sliced, and dressed with pepper and vinegar, and then thrown out, as good for nothing."

The tomato, then, was the only species in my salad eaten when its interior was ready to release sproutable seed. Ironically, that's because the tissues comprising its ovary walls now parallel much the *same* levels of nutrition and digestibility as in such sterile vegetative organs as the radish root. How is this possible?

Plants produce only seven basic kinds of tissues. Of these seven kinds only the tissue known as parenchyma exists in such quantities and has such a simple construction that humans can get a good feed by eating the cells. We eat shoots,

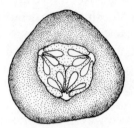

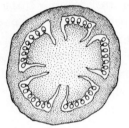

Above. Cucumber seeds cling to the inner surface of the fruit wall in three clustered, continuous rows. This *parietal* attachment is common in members of the gourd-melon family.
Below. Tomato seeds cling to a central axis dividing the fruit into four or five chambers. This *axile* attachment is common in members of the nightshade-potato family.
ILLUSTRATION BY W. W. DELANEY

roots, and fruits for their parenchyma. That's why so much vegetable cookery is devoted to learning when it's time to pick the edible organs. We lack microscopic vision, but our sense of taste allows us to choose unconsciously the period in the life of the plant organ when it contains the highest quantity of parenchyma tissue. Pick too early in development and the plant's centers of cell division (meristems) have not had time to manufacture enough parenchyma. Pick too late and the parenchyma cells may have died or their contents have been transferred and used up by neighboring, inedible tissues like fiber, wood, or protective skins.

Since parenchyma tissue is involved in the process of making food, storing it, transporting it, and secreting various substances, each parenchyma cell must contain living protoplasm. Most parenchyma cells wear only a thin, flexible, primary wall, which means that our digestive tracts are not forced to sort through thick deposits of indigestible cellulose. Parenchyma cells hang in loose clumps within the plant body, but they can exchange water, sugars, and simple minerals by extending minute threads through pits in the cell walls linking different cells together. That's what keeps salad components juicy.

Although gourmets like Brillat-Savarin went into raptures over dishes like turkey stuffed with truffles, he still wrote of salad: "It refreshes without weakening, and soothes without irritation: I often call it the renewer of youth." In fact, cell biologists know it is parenchyma that is the renewer of youth. Only one kind of plant cell has kept us hunting and gathering, gardening and harvesting, haggling and buying, peeling and chopping for thousands of years. Only one kind of plant cell allows us to extend our salad days on earth.

CHAPTER 4

Crocus Hocus-Pocus

For at the slightest touch the cakes and fruit all squirted out jets of liquid saffron, splattering our faces with the smelly stuff. Naturally enough, the use of the sacred saffron made us conclude that this course must be part of some religious rite.

Petronius, *Satyricon* (translated by W. Arrowsmith)

Has this ever happened to you? One day while shopping in a Sydney grocery store, I noticed a new display of spice packets dangling from hooks. Packets labeled SPANISH SAFFRON were for sale at the unbelievably low price of fifty cents each!

By the time I got home and examined my purchase, it was plain this was not the spice I knew. The little red bits were flat, wide, and seemed to stick together like lumps of wood pulp. Where were the long, slender, brittle threads one associates with good Spanish saffron? With increasing suspicion I emptied the entire contents of the packet into a pot of boiling water. The water promptly turned a flamingo pink instead of the expected saffron yellow and there was no pleasant odor. By the time I added the rice, even the pink tint had broken down. Linda and I had grayish, tasteless rice for dinner that night. Let the buyer beware.

Two months later, the identification desk at the Royal Botanic Garden received a visit from a pair of gentlemen working for the New South Wales Health Department. There had been complaints about some cheap spices, and one of the men opened a folder containing half a dozen familiar packets. "I'll take that!" I said with a note of enthusiasm that startled one of my coworkers. The packets were opened and the contents dumped into some vials containing a weak solution of sodium hydroxide in water. This is a standard solution for softening and clearing dried vegetable material. The stuff was allowed to soak overnight and then I examined all the pieces under the microscope.

The spice we know as saffron, Spanish saffron, or saffron threads has only one commercial source. It must come from the flowers of the saffron crocus *(Crocus sativus)*. Specifically, saffron can be derived from only one part of the flower. It comes from three threadlike stalks that dangle from the tip of the female organ of the flower.

As is characteristic of many members of the iris family (Iridaceae), the tip of the long neck of the crocus pistil subdivides into three equal, slender arms or stigmas. In many *Crocus* species the stigma tips wear delicate fringes or plumes. The stigma tips of a true saffron crocus lack most of these fine ornaments, but the stigma stalks are far longer than any known wild crocus. As the flower ages the stigma stalks dangle sloppily over the petals like three untied shoelaces.

The three stalks are a brilliant orange-red when they are alive and this color becomes more crimson when they are picked and carefully dried in a basket over a charcoal stove. It's these dried stalks that form the ready-to-use spice known as saffron threads or hay saffron. Sometimes the stalks are ground down into a powder and sold in little capsules.

Inside the dead cells of the dried stigmas is an active pigment called crocin. Crocin is one member of a huge class of

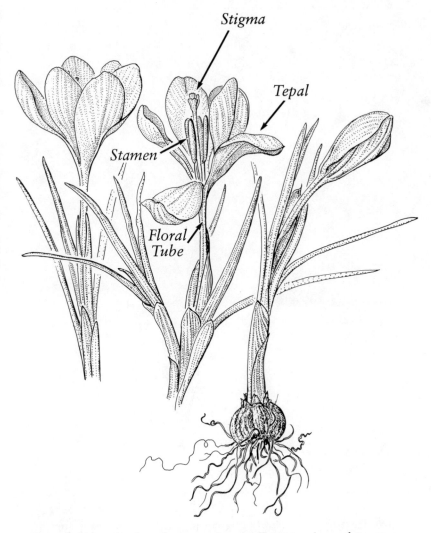

The crocus stigma is the *only* source of true saffron, so spice packets containing dried mixtures of the flower's tepals and stamens are fakes! Even so, the stigmas of these yellow crocuses *(C. flavus)* produce far too little crocin to be recommended as substitutes for stigmas of saffron crocus. ILLUSTRATION BY J. MYERS

Top. The stigma of yellow spring crocus *(C. flavus)* has short arms but broad frilled tips.

Middle. The stigma of a saffron crocus *(C. sativus)* has the longest arms but lacks showy tips.

Bottom. The arms of the *C. serotinus* stigma subdivide into delicate plumes.

ILLUSTRATION BY W. W. DELANEY

plant-made chemicals called glycosides. The crocin manufactured by the stigma of the saffron crocus is so valued because it takes only one part of this pigment to produce a strong yellow tint in one hundred thousand parts of water. The astringent scent and pleasantly bitter taste of saffron seems to be based on a related substance, called picro-crocin, sharing the same stigma cells.

A little crocin has to go a long way, since a dried-up stigma doesn't weigh much. Pharmacologists and economic botanists delight in making "gee-whiz" calculations, so it should come as no surprise that it takes at least four thousand dried stigmas to make only one ounce of saffron threads.

Saffron is not a user-friendly crop at harvesttime. The saffron gatherer visits the crocus fields every morning and gets down on his or her knees to pick whole flowers. A fresh flower is sent to a picking house, where it must be held in the left hand while the three threads are snipped off with the thumbnail on the right hand. Consequently, small quantities of saffron go for such fancy prices that threads have often been worth more than their weight in gold.

Saffron and precious metals go together, as fortunes were founded on the importation and sale of these floral organs. As guests of the Swiss Academy of Science in 1992, we scientists dined in the old Safran Haus in Basel (still owned by the now philanthropic Saffron Guild). My host pointed to the cavernous ceiling gilded with gold leaf *and* saffron powder. We raised our eyes to see a magnificent pattern of giant, stylized saffron stigmas.

Why continue to make a big fuss out of the female sex organ of a single plant? Won't any crocus do in a pinch? There are over eighty wild *Crocus* species distributed naturally from southern Europe to western China, after all. If none of them will do, why not grow saffron crocus in such large numbers that you could flood the market and bring down the price? Anyway, don't we live in an age when industrial chemistry can produce dyes that give us all shades of yellow?

If you live in the Northern Hemisphere the sight of crocuses blooming in February or March is a welcome sign that winter is ending. However, the next time you gaze fondly over these beds of spring bulbs remember that you're looking at only half the story. Many *Crocus* species flower only in autumn, and these are not popular garden plants in America. In particular, there are eight species offering white or purple flowers that refuse to pop above the soil surface until autumn begins. All eight species are native to southeastern Europe (for example, Italy, Greece, Romania, and Bulgaria), Turkey, and the Middle East. *Crocus sativus* is the most famous species in this contrary clan of fall flowers.

The saffron crocus has *never* been found far from cultivation. Its closest relative (and probable parent) is *C. cartwrightianus,* a wild autumn crocus of grassy hills and stony ground that is native to Greece and its islands. Each cell of *C. cartwrightianus* contains sixteen pairs of chromosomes. Thousands of years ago, an unknown plant of *C. cartwrightianus* produced cells containing twenty-four pairs.

The extra chromosomes changed the new plant in two important ways. First, the additional chromosomes encouraged the production of much larger flowers than its wild parent. That's why the "domesticated" saffron plant produces longer, more crocin-rich stigmas than those found in nature. Second, it looks like those extra chromosomes interfere with the normal process of seed set in cultivated saffron. Saffron flowers are almost sterile.

As so often happens, longer organs do *not* always grant superior sex. Most saffron flowers seem almost incapable of producing seed. The pollen develops abnormally. When these grains are placed on stigma tips they have a low rate of activity. Those grains producing pollen tubes often seem to "lose their way" as they grow down to the ovary, so the remaining sperm is wasted. Perhaps these pollen tubes are already too weak to go the extra distance demanded by the extra-long stigmas!

No, the only way to increase your supply of saffron is to dig up the parent stock every few years and remove the new bulbs that bud from the old. The saffron of Kashmir, Spain, and Portugal was introduced to those countries long ago by people with an eye for profit. Humans can live without saffron. The saffron crocus would become extinct without human care.

Yes, other crocuses have been grown as substitutes for saffron, but without success. It's believed that the Knights of St. John of Jerusalem introduced *C. nudiflorus,* an autumn flowerer from Spain, to England over three hundred years ago. Its threads are supposed to be almost chemically identical to those of true saffron, but *C. nudiflorus* never caught on, although the foreign plants are still found dotting the Cheshire, Sussex, Worcestershire, and Yorkshire landscapes.

The white spring crocus *(C. vernus)* has been a "substitute" of unscrupulous dealers. Dr. George E. Trease warned about this "switcheroo" in his *A Text-Book of Pharmacognosy* back in 1946. The stigmas of this garden crocus won't yield much in the way of appropriate smell or color.

Do not, under any circumstances, attempt to beat saffron prices by experimenting with look-alikes from the garden! At best, they are tasteless. At worst, they may poison you. *Colchicum autumnale* is a bulb of rock gardens and is sometimes called naked boys or stark-naked lady. However, it has often been mistaken for a true crocus due to its autumn flowering and fluted, pinkish-purple flowers. It has been sold under such names as Michaelmas crocus, autumn crocus, and "meadow saffron," but don't be fooled. Dissection reveals it's a member of the lily family (Liliaceae) and not a true crocus at all.

More important, *Colchicum* is the source of the drug colchi-

cine, and all parts of the plant appear to contain some quantity of this alkaloid. My wife, Linda, is a registered nurse, and
she explained that while colchicine is still given to gout suf-
ferers, the drug, even in small quantities, makes the patient
feel terribly nauseated. No wonder my gouty Uncle Bernie
was so cranky in his old age.

Of course, the ancient Greeks recognized these differences
and gave both the saffron and spring crocuses separate, magi-
cal origins. The crocuses of spring came out of the earth when
drops of a youth potion spilled from a cauldron cooked up by
the witch Medea. A later generation of Christians made these
flowers sacred to Saint Valentine.

The myth of the saffron crocus has much sexier connota-
tions. During the Trojan War the king and queen of heaven
quarreled bitterly over which side should win. To distract her
husband, Hera finally seduced Zeus on Mt. Ida. The saffron
crocus was one of the many wildflowers that emerged as a
result of their roll in the hay.

Saffron is probably the spice karkom, mentioned in the
Bible. It still appears in unbowdlerized versions of "The Song
of Songs" which celebrate scent and flavor to enhance love-
making. If we accept the lines of scripture literally, saffron
must have combined with things like cinnamon bark *(Cin-
namomum)*, oil rendered from roots of spikenard *(Nardo-
stachys grandiflora)*, gum from wounded branches of
frankincense *(Boswellia sacra)*, and stems of one of the
scented grasses (probably an *Andropogon*). This odorous mixture may have been applied to the skin or hair. It's also
possible it was burned as incense.

I wonder, could generations of Jewish housewives who
added these threads to the Friday soup or kneaded the powder into the Sabbath loaf have had some hidden agenda?
Saffron as an aphrodisiac seems like a rabbit's foot used as a
lucky charm. The foot was never lucky for the rabbit and, as

we've seen already, saffron threads come from a flower that can hardly be regarded as a model of potency.

It has taken a far longer time to dispel the notion that saffron is an effective medicine. The enduring belief in the West that saffron could cure almost anything can be blamed largely on a Mr. J. F. Hertodt, of Todenfeld who published a treatise on the wondrous powers of saffron back in 1670. His *Crocologia* was over two hundred pages long and insisted you could cure plague, toothaches, madness, and snakebite by combining saffron with such "goodies" as opium, mouse fat, and rotten oakwood.

Brian Mathew, of England's Royal Botanic Garden at Kew, feels there is a grain of truth in the long history of saffron cures that actually stretches back to ancient Egypt. Extracts from fresh threads reveal that they are unusually rich in vitamin B_2. Maybe so, but that hardly justifies making them into a tea and using them to treat measles, as some once recommended.

Faith in saffron has never been confined to Western Europe or even northern Africa. In 1885, a surgeon major for the Bombay army, W. Dymock, recorded the uses of saffron around Bombay. Indian physicians considered saffron to be invigorating and "preservative of the humours of the body." Yes, they also believed it was an aphrodisiac, but it was also used as a diuretic, given to induce a good sweat and believed to control difficult menstruation. The Indians appeared to have picked up the belief that saffron was good for female complaints from the people who live in the country we now know as Iran. Saffron may have the dubious distinction of being one of the earliest suppositories. Plugs of wool were dipped in a saffron solution and inserted up the unhappy orifice.

Pregnant women in Iran may have used saffron as a sort of charm to ensure a speedy delivery and expulsion of the afterbirth by hanging a saffron ball around their enlarged bellies. The balls were recorded as being as large as walnuts. Did they consist of many threads rolled together with something sticky, or balls of other substances stained with a saffron solution? If they were balls of pure threads they would have been incredibly expensive at that size.

The ancient Greeks favored saffron as a perfume and as a dyestuff. Even today we talk about saffron robes, as there was a time when cloth was stained with this costly spice. Much later, Roman emperors threw saffron threads and whole flowers to the mob as part of their triumphant processions. The Romans were most enthusiastic saffron cooks adding the spice to sauces and buns. Is it possible that the spread and influence of their empire gave the people of both conquered lands and trading partners a taste for saffron? Saffron stains and scents Spanish paella, but it is also used in a number of Italian risottos. In southern France, bouillabaisse is incomplete without saffron. In Cornwall, England, you can still buy saffron pastry around Easter. However, saffron also appears in many complicated recipes from Morocco and India in sweets and savories.

Where was saffron first grown as a crop to trade and export? Iran, southern Italy, and the coast of Syria have all been nominated. Modern plant geographers and ethnobotanists have returned to Greece and its islands, though. They point out that *C. cartwrightianus,* the wild parent of cultivated saffron, is native only to this region and still blooms around Athens. There is also strong support from archaeology. Images of crocuses in bloom have been found on pottery, hieroglyphs, tables, seal stones, and frescoes taken from excavations on the island of Crete. These artifacts date back at least to 1600 B.C. Golden pins shaped like crocus flowers have been taken from tombs.

The Cretan artists painted clustered flowers, each with

long, arching stigmas. More important, there are paintings of people actually picking crocuses and putting the flowers into bowls. Archaeologists, like Sir Arthur Evans, were convinced that Crete had once been the center of the saffron trade. One thing is for certain: Whole flowers of crocuses that look rather like saffron or wild saffron were a familiar offering to the idols of the goddesses who protected Crete and blessed its commerce. These glazed figurines often wear crocus patterns on their clay skirts.

Saffron travels well in its dormant, bulb form. Crocus bulbs, in general, lack the heavy, protective scales of lily bulbs or the layers of thick, enveloping wrappers found on onions. They make do with a comparatively light "tunic" of interwoven fibers forming nets or papery strips. Consequently, the crocus bulb is properly known as a corm. The saffron corm left Greece long ago and is not confined to Spain and Portugal. Communities in Turkey and Kashmir still attempt to grow threads as a cash crop. Saffron was once prepared in Pennsylvania (whatever happened to that industry?).

Attempts to grow saffron on a commercial scale in England can be dated back to the fourteenth century. Saffron farms were extensive between Cambridge and the aptly named Saffron Walden through the 1700s. Saffron farmers were known as crocurs or crokers. It was a difficult life as the weather of a British autumn is so unpredictable, and it's likely corms were killed by soil fungi. As crocurs had a reputation for complaining loudly, and were given to making sour predictions, some linguists think that the word *croaker* derives from *crocur.*

Of course, saffron has never been the most favored herb or spice in cuisines of English-speaking people. Can you remember the last time you tried it? Over forty years ago the gardener and plant breeder E. A. Bowles commented wryly about the tourists shopping in Cornish bakeries:

The visitors thought it the right thing to eat these bright yellow cakes and buns, but found that though they admired the colour they disliked the flavour and only bought one. So now a special brand is baked for visitors who have not acquired the taste for real Saffron, but are pleased with the colouring produced by turmeric or Safflower or some synthetic aniline dye.

I like saffron a lot but less is more. In St. Louis I purchase envelopes of saffron from any of the Italian grocery shops and delis on the side of town known as The Hill. Here is a recipe I prepare for guests.

1 or 2 saffron threads
2 cups chicken broth
1 cup rice (I prefer long grain)

Optional
Butter
Parmesan or almonds
Peas

Place the threads and broth in a heavy lidded saucepan and heat gently for at least 10 minutes (allowing the threads to stain the broth a clear gold). Heat the broth until it reaches a rolling boil, pour in the rice, cover the pot, and shake the handle gently so the rice settles evenly. Reduce heat and simmer for at least 20 minutes. Turn off the heat, remove the lid, fluff the rice with a fork, and wait about 5 minutes before serving. When you fluff up the rice you may want to add 1 tablespoon of butter with 1 or 2 tablespoons of grated Parmesan cheese or toasted almonds, or even ½ cup of shelled, freshly cooked green peas. This is nice with most lamb dishes, broiled chicken, or fish and serves as a "bed" for curry, osso buco and other meaty stews.

A trickling spring encourages the growth of blue-green algae on the beard of a tribal elder. PHOTO BY J. KELLY

Above. Few people may recognize the flowers of the caper vine, as the buds are picked and pickled long before the petals expand. These Israeli capers open their flowers at dusk to receive moths and even night-flying bees. PHOTO BY AMOS DAFNI

Left. Columbine species may hybridize in nature without man's interference. This plant had both a crimson columbine *(Aquilegia formosa)* and a Coville's columbine *(A. pubescens)* for parents.
PHOTO BY VALERIE CHASE

Thousands of years of saffron lore should be long enough to get back to that material I left soaking in a couple of vials by my lab sink. The fact is that since saffron has always been a luxury item, some people have searched for honest substitutes for ages, while others have compounded shameless frauds.

In the last century, chemical tests were first employed to expose materials posing as saffron threads. True saffron releases a blue dye if it is mixed with concentrated sulfuric acid. Improved microscopes have largely made it possible to do away with this nasty test and all the other techniques involving ether, petroleum, and alcohol.

Flowers and flower parts used to give things a yellowish tint have included the Old World marigolds *(Calendula)*, safflower *(Carthamus tinctorius)*, a South African snapdragon *(Sutera atropurpurea)*, stamens from the buttercup tree of Central America *(Cochlospermum vitifolium)*, cotton thistle *(Onopordon)*, and leopard's-bane *(Arnica montana)*. To have to make so many comparisons may sound as if I spent days working on this sample, but that was not the case. All of the plants listed above have a flower and pollen anatomy so distinct from true saffron it was like looking at the difference between human hair and feathers.

Well, what about turmeric, as it's also a yellow spice with a distinctive fragrance? Turmeric is made from the starchy underground stems of the turmeric ginger *(Curcuma longa)*, while saffron is derived from a reproductive organ. The difference between turmeric and true saffron tissues is the difference between podiatry and gynecology!

My soaked sample contained bits of flower petals, stamens, and the pollen made by those stamens. They were definitely members of the iris family. The pollen grains were oblong and had wrinkled, brainlike surfaces just like most crocus grains. There are no crocuses with red petals, so why was the dry stuff the color of blood? The New South Wales Health

Department called in an analyst. She identified the pigment as an added, red dye, Azorubine. That left me going from packet to packet looking in vain for female organs of saffron crocus. There wasn't a single one to be found! Whoever sent the stuff to Australia had most probably saved the whole crocus flowers *after* they had been picked clean of threads. The culprit(s) had cut the flowers to bits, dyed them, and rolled them up tightly to resemble threads.

Sure enough, there was a warning in the *Text-Book of Pharmacognosy*. Real saffron threads were often adulterated by mixing them with up to 50 percent stamens and other bits from the crocus flower. In my case, 100 percent of my samples consisted of petals and pollen-makers.

I sent a report of my findings to the health department officials and they seemed very pleased. I had hoped they'd call me in as an expert witness, as Australian courts have preserved so many of the quainter features of British law. I've watched some of the jurists strut their stuff outside the law courts at lunchtime still wearing their black frocks and curly white wigs. *Rumpole of the Bailey* fantasies of standing in the dock, clarifying points for a befuddled judge ("Saffron comes from a crocus flower, m'lud") and celebrating the decision over glasses of claret went through my head for weeks.

It never happened. The spice distributors pleaded guilty. The health department officials only had to prove that the contents of the spice packets had been dyed artificially. The judge was not called upon to distinguish between stamens and pistils, and the distributors were fined a thousand dollars. So the case seems to have ended on a happy note for all who attended the trial. What, you think the fine was a bit severe? Believe me, the guilty parties received the lightest of wrist taps. They wouldn't have been so lucky if the case had been tried six or seven centuries ago in medieval Nuremberg. Conviction of adulterating saffron carried the death penalty. In 1444, Jobst Findeker was burned alive with his sacks of adulterated saffron helping to fuel his fire. A dozen years later two men and a woman were buried alive for the same offense.

Consider the evidence, ladies and gentlemen of the jury. Some things can't be faked. The difference between true and false is often as basic as the difference between male and female.

CHAPTER 5

....

The Passionate Dessert

There has fallen a splendid tear
From the passion-flower at the gate.
She is coming, my dove, my dear;
She is coming, my life, my fate; . . .

Alfred, Lord Tennyson, *Maud*

Passion fruits are *not* aphrodisiacs. If the taste of one arouses you, please consider consulting a qualified psychologist. Both the common name and the scientific name *(Passiflora)* are meant to suggest an entirely different sort of passion. In fact, Catholic missionaries throughout much of the Western Hemisphere once referred to the same flower as "the Calvary Lesson."

The clerics who followed the conquistadores found passion vines both in the gardens of the native peoples of Mexico and Peru and throughout the forests of the New World tropics. Although Catholic priests extolled the rich odors and sweet flavors of the heavy fruits, some went into religious raptures after examining the conspicuous flowers on their twining stems. Here was a living example of the Lord's incarnation on earth; a perfect device to instruct heathen "Indios" into the mysteries of Christ's Passion on the cross. Of course, different missionaries sometimes interpreted the same structures in different ways.

Take both the vine's leaves and the long tendrils that enable the plant to hoist itself up rock walls and tree branches. For some, the fingerlike lobes of the leaves were the rough hands of Roman centurions binding Christ's wrists with rope (the curling tendrils). Another man felt the leaf lobes were the heads of the lances or pikes that pierced the Savior's side. The tendrils became Pilate's whip. If a priest found shiny spots on the underside of the leaves, he would say they were the thirty pieces of silver.

The missionaries were more likely to agree about the flower organs. The five sepals and five petals represented ten apostles (it was an easy matter to exclude the betraying Judas and the denying Peter). The sexual organs are mounted on top of a central post (the gynophore). That post became the column of flagellation. The five pollen-making stamens were transformed into the five wounds and the three knobby stigmas arching out from the fat ovary were the three nails of the Crucifixion.

One structure in the flower always made the good fathers ecstatic. The "column of flagellation" seemed to rise from the center of a delicate, encircling fringe. This fringe could have been a halo or the crown of thorns. Perhaps it was the actual scourge that tormented Christ. We now know that this fringe is a specialized ridge or interconnecting rim that grows out of each of the five petals. Plant anatomists call it a corona, and petal coronas are found in other garden flowers. Most daffodil or narcissus flowers have a corona too (Chapter 13), but a daff's corona forms a continuous cup while the passionflower's corona subdivides into lots of colorful threads.

Enthusiasm for the passionflower spread across the Atlantic to Rome itself. In 1610, Jacomo Bosio, author of a treatise on emblems of the Crucifixion, examined pictures of the passionflower provided by an Augustinian friar from Mexico.

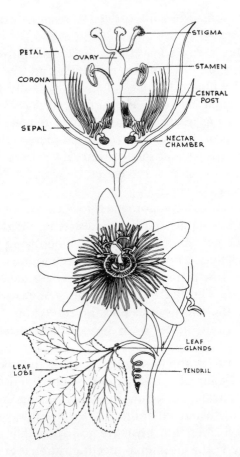

Above. By cutting through a passionflower we can see the organs that mystified the Spanish fathers. The central post is so long and erect that the plump ovary, topped with three stigmas, has the highest position in the flower. This is called a *superior* ovary or *hypogynous* flower. ILLUSTRATION BY W. W. DELANEY

Below. You can learn the Calvary Lesson combining both drawings of *P. edulis.* Lobed leaf = centurion's hand or lances; tendril = binding ropes or Pilate's whip; five sepals + five petals = ten apostles; corona = halo or crown of thorns; central post = whipping column; five stamens = five wounds; three stigmas = three nails. ILLUSTRATION BY W. W. DELANEY

Bosio announced in print that this *Flos Passionis* was the most wondrous evidence of sacred inspiration found anywhere in the world, and it seems his claim was championed by the Jesuits.

Protestant botanists were underwhelmed. Those tending passion vines in royal gardens often insisted they couldn't find the divine evidence in the flower. At least one wrote, rather sourly: "I dare say God never willed His priests to instruct His people with lies; for they come from the Devil, the author of them."

As interesting as the theological debate surrounding the plant is, what's even more fascinating is *Passiflora*'s own twisting tale of food chains. The wild *Passiflora* survives largely by offering food to animals at opportune moments. Before we look at this aspect of the passion vine, let's speculate on its origin and ecology.

The natural distribution of passion vines is most peculiar. South America is their center of diversity (over three hundred species) but a few are native to the warmer, wetter regions of Madagascar, Indonesia, Australia, and the southern parts of the United States. They are not native to Europe or tropical Africa and *all* the passion vines in Hawaii were introduced by white men.

Ecologists agree that most *Passiflora* species are "gap or gallery" plants. Consider how the canopy of a mature, tropical forest can blanket the forest floor in darkness. Not even the biggest tree can live forever. Disease, axes, earthquake, and the power of seasonal storms may combine to play the Grim Reaper. Of course, when a forest monarch comes crashing down it will take its smaller neighbors with it. This punches a large light gap in the canopy umbrella. Tree seedlings that have remained in stunted conditions for years bolt for the sun, but it may take years for a couple of saplings to "plug up the hole in the forest's roof." During that period the gap belongs to fast-growing "weed" trees, vines, and thickets whose seeds arrived in the dung of birds and bats or blew in on the wind.

The ability of passion vines to blanket disturbed patches remains one of the few saving graces in this sad century of tropical destruction. It amazes me how some species can take hold even on some of the most eroded sites. Nothing softens the impact of barbed-wire fences throughout Central America like wild passion vines hanging blue flowers over rusty hooks.

You don't even have to visit the tropics to see the scrambling advance of the passion vines. In the more southerly parts of the United States our own yellow maypop *(Passiflora lutea)* and the apricot vine *(P. incarnata)* ramble along shady roadsides, railroads, fence rows, old pastures—wherever we've cleared away strips of the standing forest.

Passion vines do not sprawl in peace while the gap lasts. For much of their lives they must combat the most implacable of enemies that will reduce the most luxuriant stems to a few dry sticks. These squirming predators arrived as eggs laid by an insect with almost instinctive cunning. I refer to the aggressive caterpillars that are transformed into the common, beautifully banded *Heliconius* butterflies of the New World tropics.

If *Heliconius* larvae don't find enough passion leaves they'll eat each other! I watched these cannibal caterpillars from hell during my Peace Corps days in El Salvador. While botanizing on a volcanic slope I found climbing stems of bat leaf passionflower *(P. coriacea)* wearing the cutest, spiniest, white caterpillars. I brought three larvae and two stems back to my lab. In two days the caterpillars had eaten the last bat leaf. The smallest caterpillar vanished first, leaving only a bit of hairy skin. The biggest caterpillar ate the medium-size one the following week. The survivor had acquired enough protein to turn into a jewellike chrysalis. Unfortunately, the butterfly emerged over the weekend when my windows were locked, and I returned to find a pretty black-and-yellow corpse. Serves him right!

Passiflora species have cyanide-based toxins in their leaves. This may slow the caterpillar's rapid rate of growth and limit the number of *Heliconius* species that can devour the same species of passion vine. However, the most successful caterpillars never sicken and actually accumulate "passion poisons" in their own bodies making them distasteful to birds.

Fooling the pregnant butterfly is another way to avoid her juvenile delinquents. *P. cyanea* wears two golden, egglike structures on its leaves. To a female *Heliconius* they may resemble two butterfly eggs ready to hatch and she will not deposit her own offspring on such leaves. Other scientists have suggested that the variable leaf shapes of passion vines may mimic the foliage of common tropical plants that *Heliconius* larvae find inedible. Female butterflies may not locate a suitable passion vine if its leaves are camouflaged to resemble, say, the leaves of a cecropia tree.

Most *Passiflora* species may avoid becoming caterpillar food by actually offering food to the caterpillars' enemies. Look at the leaves of most passion vines. The leaf stalk (petiole) is often studded with fat, round bumps. These bumps are really nectar glands secreting a sweet fluid that is often very rich in amino acids. Ants and tiny parasitic wasps or flies drink the nectar. Ants accustomed to investigate passion vines will regularly kill and eat the youngest phases of the *Heliconius* caterpillars. Wasps lay their eggs on the older, plumper larvae.

Biting a passion leaf may be a dangerous vocation, and it looks like the most successful passion vine "bites" the caterpillar first. *P. adenopoda* wears a thick coat of tough hairs. The caterpillar egg hatches out on the stem but the larva doesn't move very far, as it becomes lashed down by hairy hooks.

Struggling to free itself, the caterpillar's body is lacerated by the sharp barbs tipping each hair until the insect bleeds to death.

When passion vines come into bloom the flowers must also offer food for services rendered. It's another variation on the nectar-for-pollen-transport tale, but now we can see the function of the bizarre corona. The corona seems to have at least two roles in the life of the flower. First, the corona helps to advertise the flower's presence in most *Passiflora* species. It is usually a contrasting color to that of the petals and sepals, and it may be brilliantly banded. This is an obvious visual cue to pollinators flying by.

More important, though, is that the corona acts as a sort of barrier or screen to protect the nectar secreted at the base of the petal tube. The corona screen prevents the entrance of unsuitable insects, like tiny bees and flies, which would steal nectar without contacting the sexual organs mounted on the central post. The nectar in the flower is only for animals strong enough, large enough, or heavy enough to pull away the screen and ram their heads past the tangle of corona threads.

Passionflowers tend to lead short lives in the fast lane. Within twelve hours or less, most flowers will crumple into limp, sticky rags whether their ovary has been fertilized or not. Cross-pollination is often essential for fruit-set. Some blossoms seem to be sperm junkies and will not even start a fruit until nearly two hundred pollen grains stick to the three knobby tips of each pistil.

Naturalists rising shortly before dawn have commented on the amazing speed at which a bud literally pops open. Within ten seconds to a minute the sepals and petals have spread apart and the sexual organs have cocked themselves at the correct angles to contact incoming pollinators. What pollinates a passionflower? That seems to depend on the flower's size and mode of advertising. At one end of the scale we have

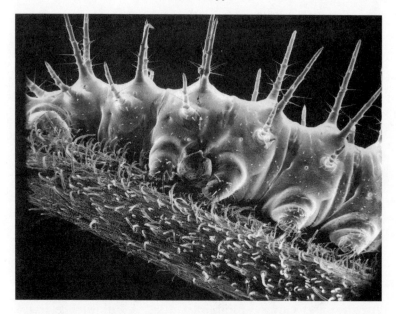

Fearsome spines worn by a *Heliconius* caterpillar are no protection from the sharp, hooked hairs on the stems of *Passiflora adenopoda*. These vine hairs trapped and stabbed the larva until it died of a combination of starvation and bleeding. PHOTO BY DR. L. GILBERT

passion vines that make little greenish flowers that have a diameter smaller than a pinky nail and form shallow bowls. They have a musky odor and seem to depend largely on short-tongued wasps. At the other end we have large, stiff, scarlet flowers that are two to five inches across and have petal tubes forming long cylinders. These flowers have no obvious smell but they are pollinated by both long-billed and hermit hummingbirds that probe between the corona threads and are alert to red-orange colors, not scent.

The most remarkable passionflower belongs to *P. mucronata* from the coast of southeastern Brazil. It opens between one and two A.M. and has usually collapsed by mid-morning. Pale green, white, and cream in color, it's al-

most four inches across. Its night fragrance is weak but sam-
plers insist it's reminiscent of fresh pumpkin, or raw green
beans, or even lemon cake. The petal tube forms a wide cup.
The dominant pollinators are two species of long-tongued
bats. The bat shoves its tongue down into the floral cup while
it hovers in the air for a moment, just like a hummingbird!

The flowers of the majority of *Passiflora* species fit somewhere in the middle of the wasp-bird/bat extremes. Their
flowers are as round as large coins and they come in vivid
colors, often combining blue, purple, and yellow. Some have
such sweet perfumes that naturalists have compared them to
the fragrances of cultivated carnations. Such passion vines
advertise their flowers for the benefit of many different kinds
of tropical bees. Carpenter bees (xylocopids) may be among
the most important pollinators.

I've watched big carpenters on so many different flowers
over the years and have dismissed them for their obesity, bass
buzzing, and clumsy, fumbling antics. A bumblebee has a
quiet charm and sylphlike grace compared to the coarseness
of carpenters. Well, looks can be deceiving. It turns out that
carpenter bees are courteous shoppers and devoted home-
makers. Passionflowers may bring out their best behavior.
After a female carpenter drinks the nectar in the floral cup of
the apricot vine, she will not leave the flower until she marks
it with a perfume secreted from a gland on her own body.
When another carpenter bee lands on the same flower she is
repelled by the "perfume mark," and carpenter bees avoid a
marked flower for up to ten minutes. Dr. Gordon Frankie and
S. B. Vinson have suggested that the bee has left a chemical
sign on the passionflower that reads, "Don't waste your time,
sister, I've emptied this blossom."

When the bee flies home to her burrow, does she give the
nectar to her children, as is? No, she sits in the entrance to her
nest and carefully regurgitates the nectar of yellow maypop.
The sun "cooks" the drop evaporating some of the water so

the sugar concentration of the nectar increases over 20 percent. When the nectar reaches the right syrupy consistency,
mother carpenter mixes it with pollen to make a "loaf" or
"pudding," and only then is it fit for her offspring.

If the pistil of a passionflower has been fertilized, it may still
take a month or so before it swells into a ripe fruit. Passion
fruits "signal" their ripeness when greenish skins change
color. The colors and sizes of passion fruit may be as broad as
the colors of their flowers. Some of the wild Central American
species adopt the shiny blackness and shape of a Greek olive.
The fruit of the weedy bombillo, or "love-in-a-mist" *(P. foe-
tida)*, is a bit larger but turns bright red. Midway between a
Ping-Pong and tennis ball is the maracuja, or Nelly Kelly *(P.
edulis)*, which turns a lustrous purple with bronze flushes.
The giant granadilla *(P. quadrangularis)* may wear its common name with pride, as its fruit often resembles a football.
Its skin turns the sort of lurid yellow you see in old Tech-
nicolor movies. Overripe fruit develops a clammy, wrinkled
rind that has the disconcerting feel of old meat.

Cut open any ripe passion fruit and you will see that each
seed is wrapped in its own juice sack. These sacks are attached
in clusters directly to the fruit wall in three distinct clumps.
The easiest way to eat a fresh passion fruit is to divide it into
two equal halves and scrape out the juice sacks with a teaspoon as if you were eating a soft-boiled egg. Yes, the seeds
can be swallowed whole or crunched, as they are perfectly
harmless. Just keep a napkin ready, because the pigments in
the rind can stain clothing.

That's why most people living in Latin America call passion
fruits *granadillas* (many little seeds). The conquering Span-
iards compared the passion fruit to the seedy fruit of Old
World *grenadillas* or pomegranates *(Punica granatum)*. The
passion fruit and the pomegranate are so unrelated, though,
that they are placed in separate families.

Passion vines with fruit lure man into the tropical web of

the eaters and the eaten. When I learned how good commercial passion fruits could taste I thought I'd munch my way through the forests of Central America. Unfortunately, the fruit of many wild species is strictly for the birds, or bats, or monkeys. The pulp was often insipid and watery.

Passion fruit as people food is often limited to only two choices: the giant granadilla and the Nelly Kelly. They're sweet enough, mind you, but their seeds are rather gritty. I long for the day when there's a commercial market for the sweet granadilla, or curuba *(P. ligularis),* in America and Australia. It's the size of a goose egg and wears "Easter egg" colors of red, yellow, and green flecks. This was the most common passion fruit sold throughout Central America. The pulp is positively ethereal but even the seeds are delicious, as they have soft shells and nutty centers. They are now growing this species in Hawaii so perhaps I won't have to wait too long.

A panel of the National Research Council in Washington has identified forty species of edible passion fruits native to the tropical Americas. The panel insists that the tastiest fruits are passing us by and we should be encouraging the breeding and cultivation of species known to those people still scratching a living from the Peruvian Andes. An industry based on passion fruit was introduced to Puerto Rico in 1976. The island now exports three thousand tons of the fruit annually netting a total of over ten million dollars. Passion vines can be generous producers, so the fruit is an inexpensive treat when in season. At the time I write this sentence (June 1992), Nelly Kellys sell five for a dollar in Sydney markets.

Passion fruits can be cooked. The Maka Indians of Paraguay bake unripe fruits of how-how *(P. mooreana)* on hot stones. This seems a bit extreme—I'd rather wait for the fruit to sweeten through ripening. Passion fruit keeps you cool through much of Central America. The pulp is scooped out, mixed with water (or milk) and sugar, and then blended into a tall drink, or *refresco.* You can buy granadilla ice cream or sherbets at most Central American *sorbeterías*. The pulp may be mixed with enough sugar to make a stiff fruit paste that can be served at the end of a meal with a dollop of cream cheese and a cup of bitter coffee. I understand that Brazilians use the rind of the giant granadilla to make marmalade, but have never sampled it myself.

Although the Nelly Kelly also hails from Brazil, it is grown throughout warmer regions of New Zealand and Australia. The fruit is so firmly clasped to the antipodal breast that passion vines rambling over trellises and sheet-metal fences are sights common to both cities and small towns. In the first half of this century, "down under" cooks beat them into pastry icings, used them to flavor sago puddings, and layered the pulp in cake and gelatin trifles. Fruit salads were incomplete without lots of fresh pulp.

A cottage industry for passion-fruit conserves has made an Australian comeback in both the gourmet shops of exclusive suburbs and the roadside stands of country orchards. By mixing passion-fruit pulp with the lighter flesh of other fruits the dark seeds shimmer in a bright jam. Clever marketing pushes the product. Passion fruit cooked with tomato juice becomes "ladybird jelly." When combined with lemons the label may read "leopard marmalade." As the world shrinks, Australian dishes calling for passion fruit have become increasingly innovative. The juice is recommended for both dessert soufflés and in dressings that go over complex salads calling for avocado and smoked Tasmanian trout!

Passion fruit plays its most noble role in the completion of the dessert called pavlova. It's here we get into very dangerous territory, though, as both Australia and New Zealand have heated claims to being the birthplace of the first pavlova. To confuse matters even more, the first time I was served pavlova was back in El Salvador in 1975. The family with whom I boarded were of French-Italian stock and they knew that pavlovas were the most civilized way of serving granadillas.

As the name suggests, the pavlova is supposed to commemorate the great ballerina Anna Pavlova, who made two tours of the antipodes before 1930. "As light as Pavlova" was the highest compliment you could pay a dessert. It takes little imagination to look at this soft meringue dressed in whipped cream and crowned with passion fruit to see a dancer in a white tutu and jeweled tiara.

Recommending the best recipe for pavlova is another minefield. Every cook in Australia or New Zealand is convinced he or she knows the *only* right way to make pavlova. As this is not a cookbook, I can at least preserve domestic harmony and give my wife's favorite version, which she modified from Maureen Simpson's *Australian Cuisine* (Sydney: ABC Enterprises, 1990).

PAVLOVA BAKED ON THE PLATE
(Serves 6–8 people)

6 egg whites from the largest, freshest eggs available
pinch of salt
1 heaping cup of granulated white sugar
1 teaspoon white vinegar (some prefer malt vinegar)
1 ½ tablespoons white cornflour
1 teaspoon vanilla extract
1–2 cups whipping cream
3–4 passion fruits
6 strawberries
4–5 slices kiwi fruit

Preheat the oven to 400 degrees F. Grease your largest ovenproof plate on which you want to serve the finished pavlova and dust with some excess flour. Beat the egg whites with the salt until stiff. Add the sugar one heaping tablespoon at a time. Once all the sugar has been added, the mixture should be thick and shiny. Stir in the vinegar, cornflour, and vanilla. Pile the mixture onto the center of the plate until you have a rough, rounded mound about 2½ inches high (ensures a good marshmallowy center). Just before placing the pavlova in the oven, turn down the heat to 250 degrees; bake for 1½ to 1¾ hours.

The finished meringue should swell up dramatically in the oven and its crust will crack. Once it is removed from the oven, though, it will deflate. (To prevent it from becoming too flabby, Linda turns off the oven, opens the door about halfway, and lets the pavlova "proof" about 10 to 20 minutes as the oven cools. By the way, Linda thinks the "perfect pav" should really be baked in a spring pan lined with greased ovenproof paper. She doesn't proof the pav until after it's cool enough to remove its metal "corset.") Whipped cream and fruit are added to the cooled meringue just before you are ready to serve.

How you add the passion fruit may also define national bias. New Zealanders, one observes, prefer to fold well-separated pulp *into* the whipped cream. They think pulp on the surface is ugly, as it looks like frog eggs. Australians prefer to scatter the pulp on top of the cream so it glistens among the slices of strawberries and kiwi fruit.

We've had great success serving pavlova to guests at the end of a traditional Thanksgiving dinner. If you tell diners it's only egg whites and fresh fruit they'll think it's a health food and greedily demand seconds.

PART THREE

Scientific Obsessions

CHAPTER 6

Thrilled by Thrums

These brilliant hues are all distinct and clean,
No kindred tints, no blending streaks between,
This is no shaded, run-off, pin-eyed thing:
A king of flowers, a flower for England's king.

George Crabbe, *The Borough*

Scientists studying sections of the Konza Prairie, in the Flint Hills of Kansas, plan their experimental fires with care. Fire clears away the straw and thatch that accumulates each season and stimulates tender growth for buffalo and deer. "Burning off" in March or early April doesn't endanger wildlife, since most ground birds have not started laying eggs and small animals have not emerged from their safe winter burrows.

Last March the wind changed suddenly and a fire went briefly out of control. The flames ran free long enough to rush down the hillside and burn my plot. It's May now and the underground stems of tallgrasses poke above the ashen soil looking like gnarled, charred fingers. They are not dead but burning has delayed their spring shoots.

Smoking winds, like dark clouds, have silver linings. The grasses suffer temporarily but their loss encourages many spring herbs that overwintered as tubers or bulbs. Smaller wildflowers rarely have a chance to display all their spring charms, since they are hidden by the burgeoning grass or smothered under thatch. The violet wood sorrel *(Oxalis violacea)* is never higher than my heel, yet it's running riot over the plot forming dense tufts and patchworks.

I kneel down, look into the cup of each flower with a hand lens, and take notes. The violet wood sorrel produces two different forms of flowers, but each plant produces only one form. More than half of the plants have flowers in which the five necks (styles) of each pistil fill up the entrance to the petal tube with their fat, knobby tips (stigmas). Their pollen-making stamens are so short you can't even see them, since the fat stigmas block the flower's tube.

The remaining plants have flowers in which thick, long stamens fill up the flower's tube to release their yellow pollen. To see the short pistil necks in this flower you have to pick off the petals. The fat stigmas have such short necks that they must "squeeze" between the outer stalks of two rows of stamens to expose their receptive tips.

It's getting chilly and the smell of scorched earth is still so strong it gives me a headache. Soot gets into my sneakers and blackens my knees. Linda will give me the silent treatment because I promised to take her into town for dinner and a movie half an hour ago. She has no idea that for the first time in my career I am sharing secrets with Charles Darwin.

Back in 1877 Charles Darwin published a fat book with a long title: *The Different Forms of Flowers on Plants of the Same Species.* This work takes a careful look at how plants have altered their breeding systems by modifying the organs making up each flower. Within these pages we find flowers that never open their petals and pollinate themselves in the bud (cleistogamous means closed-marriage flowers). There are Darwin's "polygamous plants" in which a single twig may bear both a bisexual (perfect) flower and a couple of unisex-

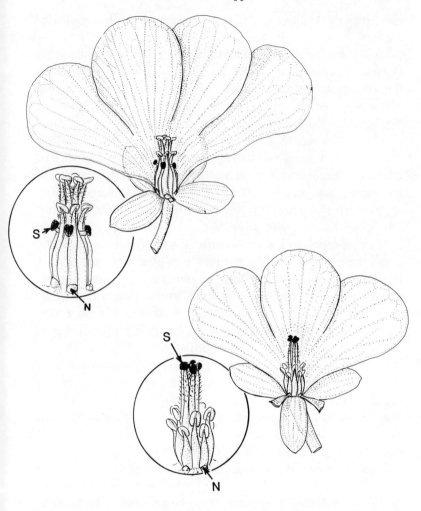

There are two flower forms in pink wood sorrel (a third form was "lost" over time).

Above. Flowers on some plants have pistil necks so short that their knobbed tips (*S* is for stigma) poke between the longer stamen stalks.

Below. Remaining plants have pistil necks so long they tower over the stamen cluster. To reach the nectar (*N* is for nectary) an insect crawls *between* the petal tube and the sexual organs. ILLUSTRATIONS BY J. MYERS

ual (imperfect) flowers that can make only pollen grains *or* seeds.

Wood sorrels play an important part in his book, although Darwin concentrated on species from southern Africa. Their flowers always contain both stamens *and* pistils. There are often two (we will sometimes find three) flower forms in a population of wood sorrels. Darwin called them heterostylous plants (*hetero* means different; *stylous* means pistil necks).

It's easy to see that such a book would have a sort of scholarly charm and remain important to professors and professional plant breeders, but Darwin's work captured a large segment of the general public. *The Different Forms of Flowers* has gone through several editions.

For me, much of Darwin's genius comes from his talent for using the most common creatures to explain complex topics. He enlisted domestic pigeons to illustrate how new species may evolve, and the bird in the city gutter was as important to his model system as the fanciest fantail in her dovecote. Darwin did not take his English audience through the rigors of heterostyly until he had reintroduced them to one of their favorite flowers, the primrose. Darwin literally lures his readers up the primrose path discussing the strange yet familiar sex life of such British primroses as the milkmaid or May spink *(Primula vulgaris)*, cowslip *(P. veris)*, and oxlip *(P. elatior)*, and such prized foreigners as the auricula *(P. auricula)* and Chinese primrose *(P. sinensis)*.

Darwin must have known that the sentimental feelings of his audience would help him get his points across. Centuries of English folklore, literature, and plant breeding had conditioned middle-class Victorians to be passionate about primroses. Wild primroses flowered so early in the season that they were regarded as "ambassadors of spring" (from the medieval Latin: *prima* means first; *rosa* means rose or blossom). Some rural people may have still believed that primrose remedies could cure arthritis, close wounds, stop convulsions, remove wrinkles, restore lost speech, and make bashful men stop blushing. Fresh primroses were still gathered by cooks to make a liqueur called cowslip wine, or strung together by nannies to give children a scented plaything called a totsie ball.

Primrose superstitions had great charm. The nightingale sang only where cowslips flourished. Pick a primrose and bring it into the house and you angered spirits who cursed your ducklings and laying hens. British poets never stopped insisting that primroses were fairy flowers. Queen Victoria sent Prime Minister Disraeli bouquets of primroses from her wooded estates and the PM thanked his queen by writing that her flowers were "an offering from the Fauns and Dryads of Osborne."

More important, Darwin's book must have appealed to the many people who bred primroses for competition. In the last century the word *florist* did *not* refer to a shopkeeper who sold cut flowers. A real florist grew certain flowers to reach the highest standard of excellence and then exhibited his handiwork at florists' feasts (usually held at inns) to win recognition and prizes. Breeds based on the auricula *(P. auricula)* of the Alps and the polyanthus (garden hybrids between *P. vulgaris* and *P. veris*) were always the most popular. Contests for best primroses were especially popular through the counties of northern England, which saw more than fifty shows organized annually as early as 1826.

Darwin used the language of the hobbyist. If all the flowers on the primrose had stubby stamens inserted low on the petal tube and a long pistil neck with a swollen tip, then the grower called it a pin-eyed plant. The rounded stigma, "peeking out" of the floral tube, really does look like a decorative pinhead or brooch.

On the other hand, if the flowers had flat-tipped, short-necked pistils concealed under long stamens forming a dense, yellow ring at the top of the tube, then the gardener

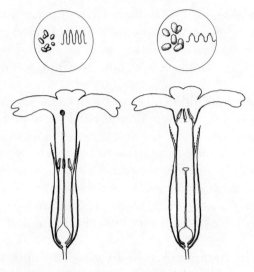

Left. The pin flower of a primrose has a pistil with a *long* neck ending in a *swollen* tip composed of long, narrow cells. The stamens are located *inside* the petal tube and produce *small* pollen grains.

Right. The thrum flower has a pistil with a *short* neck ending in a *flattened* tip composed of short, broad cells. The stamens are located *outside* the "mouth" of the petal tube and produce *large* pollen grains. ILLUSTRATION BY W. W. DELANEY

owned a thrum-eyed plant. What's a thrum? It seems to be an old weaver's term for the stray ends of threads hanging off a loom. The tight ring of pollen-making anthers on the top of a thrum flower must have reminded someone of a tuft of yarn.

Darwin, like a Shakespearean sprite, entered the cowslip's bell but then pulled the reader in with him as if he were guiding him through a factory. Experiments made the function of the floral equipment much easier to understand. A pin flower would not make seed if pollinated with its own grains. It couldn't even set seed if the pollen came from another pin flower on a completely different plant. The same held true for the thrum. Nature obviously hated continual self-fertilization and the evolution of heterostyly allowed most primroses to avoid inbreeding.

A bee or butterfly lands on a pin flower and pokes its tongue deep into the petal tube to gather nectar at the blossom's base. The probing tongue rubs against the stubby anthers deep within the tube. When the same insect flies to a thrum flower, the pin grains are transferred to the pistil tip hidden deep inside its tube. Conversely, cross-pollination must also occur when the insect's head contacts the exposed anther ring on a thrum and it brings the same thrum pollen to the knobby pistil rising out of the pin-flower's tube.

This sexual tit-for-tat must have amused the primrose lover, but then Darwin surprised his readers by showing how common this system was in the field, garden, and greenhouse. It appeared in the wood sorrels of Africa and in such "down home" plants as the European flaxes *(Linum)*, lungwort *(Pulmonaria)*, and bogbeans *(Menyanthes)*. Since Darwin's day species in about twenty-four families of flowering plants have been found to have heterostylous flowers.

Darwin also showed that it was possible for individuals in the same population to have three different forms of flowers. Evocative names like pin and thrum didn't quite work here, so Darwin simply called the three stereotyped forms long-, mid-, and short-styled (and so they remain today). Three flower forms (tristyly) occur far less frequently in nature compared to the pin and thrum (distyly) system. Modern botanists record tristyly in only four flowering families. Most African wood sorrels have flowers with three breeding forms, but Darwin noted the same condition in the common loosestrife or butterfly weed *(Lythrum)* of British ponds and marshes.

Pottering around with the violet wood sorrel feeds my ego. It lets me become an honorary runner in a scientific torch race that started with Charles Darwin. Those who followed Darwin have become almost obsessed with heterostyly. We know such blossoms have something special to contribute to the study of how a plant population functions in the real world.

You see, since these flower forms "breed true" they have served as dependable systems for clarifying the mathematical rules behind inheritance and evolutionary change. Some of the most perceptive biologists of this century have turned to heterostylous plants, but I'll never really fit into this brilliant club, as its members, like Darwin, are almost always British. Does the "lure" of pin and thrum reach them in their cradles? For example, prior to the Second World War R. A. Fisher (the father of biostatistics) used the inheritance of flower forms in loosestrife to develop models for predicting rates of change in populations. A few decades later, Professor E. B. Ford examined rural primroses to see how breeding forms could be lost as local habitats altered with time. For the past fifteen years or so, Dr. Spencer Barret has studied the frequency of flower forms in the water hyacinth *(Eichhornia crassipes)* as this floating weed reaches plague proportions.

Breeding experiments combined with careful comparisons of flower structure offer thrilling evidence that heterostyly is controlled by only a couple of genes. Pin and thrum systems seem to function happily with a single S gene. When a pin flower crosses with a thrum, half the seeds grow into pin plants and half into thrums. Species that offer three flower forms are a bit more complicated and must operate with both an S and M gene (no comments, please).

The range of features controlled by just one or two genes operating in the same flower is often enormous. One or two genes can determine the size, shape, surface sculpture, color, and starchiness of each pollen grain. The *same* gene or genes may determine the hairiness of the pistil, the length of each pistil neck, and both the "chunkiness and knobbiness" of the pistil tip. The *same* gene or genes control the diameter of the petal tube and the hairs lining that tube. You have to look very closely, though, to see what a gene can do. Pin and thrum systems have evolved so often in so many unrelated families of plants that the S gene's influence changes markedly from group to group. For example, in the pin flowers of my wood sorrels the pistil necks wear dense clumps of prickly hairs. The pistil necks in the pin flowers of most other plants with heterostylous flowers are quite bald by comparison.

Scientists stay "hooked on heterostyly" because we still have not quite figured out what it's all for. Sure it encourages cross-pollination but, if it's so efficient, why don't all the flowers on this planet have it? In fact, the arrangement between pins and thrums is far from equal in some species, like the violet wood sorrel. Out on the prairie, my pin plants made more flowers and set far more seed than the thrums.

Furthermore, pin and thrum systems are not equally distributed throughout the world. Why is this breeding system so common throughout Eurasia and North America but so rare in local vegetation of other parts of the world? Few species of Australian plants show any sign of heterostyly, while the same condition is a "familiar trademark" of the shrubs and wildflowers of southern Africa.

I share some theories with my British "betters" but can't prove them . . . yet. Heterostyly seems most likely to evolve in insect-pollinated flowers that are already equipped with long tubes, funnels, or deep cups. The insects that regularly visit pin and thrum blossoms seek out and sip nectar avidly but they seem less likely to scrape sexual organs for pollen. Any bee netted on the pink wood sorrel carried few grains in her pollen baskets (twenty grains was a big "shopping load") and she wore the lightest sprinkling of grains on her head and back. Perhaps heterostyly is just a mechanism designed to transfer flower sperm to insects that are frequent visitors but the daintiest of drinkers.

One of the most exciting features of pin and thrum systems is that they can change so quickly. The flower forms remain pretty balanced in stable, unchanging environments. When something makes the environment more stressful or the plants start migrating into new territories, one or more flower forms may change. The wood sorrels, in particular, provide evidence of how easily natural selection may change or suppress the original forms of flowers over time.

The violet wood sorrels of Konza should have three flower forms, as do related species in Mexico and South America. Botanists have looked for the missing third form on midwestern prairies and woodlands for more than a century without success. The ancestors of my plants appear to have migrated north from Mexico to "homestead" the grasslands of the United States. As these pioneers encountered cooler and shorter growing seasons they "discarded" their mid-style forms like heavy furniture cast off a covered wagon to lighten the load.

Somewhere on the dark forest floors of Oregon and Washington State a wood sorrel may be eliminating one of its three flower forms even as I type. The mid-style flowers of Suksdorf's wood sorrel *(Oxalis suksdorfii)* produce almost no seeds and they don't produce enough grains to compete for fatherhood with their long- and short-style siblings. It's possible that future generations of naturalists will gather the yellow flowers and know this wood sorrel only as a pin and thrum species.

There reaches a point, though, when the flower forms have become so altered that true heterostyly vanishes. Switch off the S and M genes and you are left with many yellow sorrels well adapted to suburban life-styles. Check out the bare spots on your lawn or the narrow strips under the hedges. You should find the little yellowish blooms of ladies' sorrel *(O. corniculata)* or toad sorrel *(O. stricta)*. They grow fast, self-pollinate, set seed, and die like any seasonal weed. Sometimes the flowers don't even bother opening and there is a "closed marriage" in the buds. Quantity without quality, perhaps, but such weedy sorrels are now found all over the world and should persist as long as people garden.

What do you think would happen if you dug up a single flower form of a heterostylous plant and grew it in another part of the world? You would expect that one flower form could not be expected to set seed in the absence of its breeding mates and the lone form would die out without continued coddling. You're only half right. The plant *would* have a tough time making seeds, but gardeners have learned to their chagrin that some wood sorrels can survive without sex.

Southern Africa has the largest and most beautiful yellow-, white-, or purple-flowered wood sorrels. They produce tough, bulblike structures that can be yanked out, shipped overseas, and then planted again like daffodils or tulips. The bulbs make more bulbs as they grow older and fatter, and they spread out and under the soil, choking preferred plants in their path.

Only one of the flower forms of *Oxalis pes-caprae* left South Africa late in the eighteenth century under the deceptive name of Bermuda buttercup (it's not native to Bermuda). Few people living outside South Africa have ever seen it produce ripe capsules. Nevertheless, it first escaped from Sicilian gardens as early as 1796 and is now well on its way to being declared a noxious pest in many countries with warm, dry climates. Travelers have been continually seduced by the pale yellow flowers and have carried the little bulbs to foreign lands, where they have escaped in turn. Under its more appropriate name of soursob, *O. pes-caprae* now spreads through most of the Mediterranean basin, parts of India and New Zealand, and is doing its best to eat up the arable lands of southern Australia. It has invaded the artichoke fields and citrus groves of California. To quote a recent writer on weeds, soursob is "greeted almost with despair anywhere."

Life abroad suits the sexless life-style of soursob, since it lacks natural enemies outside South Africa. The acidic plants are rich in potassium oxalate. Sheep that dine too often on soursob die of kidney failure.

Heterostylous plants deserve our respect and demand our attention. As their methods of reproduction shift, they impart an old but valuable lesson we shouldn't forget. There can be no survival of the fittest unless the fittest proves reproductively fit.

CHAPTER 7

Something with Poison in It*

". . . you may observe a Bread-and-butter-fly. Its wings are thin slices of bread-and-butter, its body is a crust, and its head is a lump of sugar."

"And what does *it* live on?"

"Weak tea with cream in it."

A new difficulty came into Alice's head. "Supposing it couldn't find any?" she suggested.

"Then it would die, of course."

"But that must happen very often," Alice remarked thoughtfully.

"It always happens," said the Gnat.

Lewis Carroll, *Through the Looking Glass*

What was wrong with this honeybee? Worker bees *(Apis mellifera)* always seem to be such predictable models of efficiency. They start at the lowest flower on a stem and climb upward in a continuous spiral while poking their tongues into each blossom along the way. Once the worker makes it to the tip of the stem, or the last open flower, she flutters down to the base of the next-closest stem and repeats the process. It's an energy-saving technique, as climbing up burns fewer calories than flying up.

*Dedicated to the memory of Irene Baker

My honeybee had lost her sense of direction. She back-tracked and wandered about, losing the spiral pattern. She made staggering and jittery motions with her legs as she climbed. Her tongue was extended and retracted in weird spasms. Sometimes the bee aimed her tongue in the air and sometimes her tongue completely missed the interior of the flowers and began licking the flower's stalk instead. When I dropped the butterfly net over the whole plant, she made no attempt to fly away. I usually feel a twinge of regret when I drop any insect into a cyanide jar. *This* was a mercy killing.

Over the next two weeks in May I'd collect many more honeybees that were foraging on the wildflowers of the Konza Prairie Research Natural Area of Kansas. Those bees display-ing the same set of symptoms as the first victim were observed only on *Zigadenus nuttallii.* There are about fifteen *Zigadenus* species in North America and they have many common names, but if you're a stockman or ranch owner, you call these creamy white flowers death camas, crow poison, black snakeroot, or poison sego. A copy of *American Honey Plants,* a classic work of natural history written in 1920 by Frank C. Pellett, confirmed my suspicions. Pellett had described how honeybees returned to their hives to die after taking nectar in fields of death camas, "sometimes in alarming numbers." To solve the mystery, though, we have to answer two questions. What is nectar? How does it differ from the honey in beehives?

The Roman poet Virgil seems to have been the first author to call the sweet liquid in a flower *nectar,* after the beverage of the immortal gods. Scientists have preserved Virgil's poetic vision. The ancients believed that a flower's nectar came di-rectly from heaven. Drops of firmament fell into waiting cups and bowls made of petals, or were placed there by deities like Iris, the divine messenger and rainbow goddess. All the bees had to do was gather up these heavenly drops and "ripen" them in wax combs as honey. That's why Roman naturalists, like Pliny, called honey "the saliva of the stars."

Over the centuries this belief was modified a bit. The supernatural did not have to intervene. Nectar was seen as dew, mist, or raindrops that had seeped into flowers. If rain was so refreshing to the dry earth it must have some sort of inherent sweetness. Most men of science stuck by this belief until less than four centuries ago. Today we understand that flowers are designed to avoid accumulating water directly from the atmosphere. Flowers avoid soaked interiors based on the time and temperature at which they bloom, their coats of water-resistant hairs, and by the protective angles they hold to avoid splashes. If rain or dew still leaks into a flower, it dilutes the nectar instead of enriching it.

The invention of powerful lenses made it possible for botanists to closely examine the surface of a flower, revealing a concealed world of moist bumps, discs, and crowns. The Dutch botanist Carolus Clusius was probably the first to describe nectar glands, back in 1601 after examining the flowers of a crown imperial *(Fritillaria imperialis)*, a relative of the death camas. He found "little tubercles" on the petals that "exude drops of clear, sweet water resembling tears."

Nectar, then, is the sweet, water-based fluid secreted by a gland called a nectary. However, it took centuries of experiments, debate, and wounded reputations before most botanists would agree, almost grudgingly, that nectar is an edible reward made *by* a flower *for* its pollinators. In fact, most of the earliest investigators insisted loudly and aggressively that functional nectaries excreted "waste" products, or a bath for flower sperm, or a lubricant to loosen "tight" petals, or a "sap" to feed baby seeds, and so on. These physiologists tended to treat the few field naturalists observing flower-insect interplay with undisguised contempt. Let's not laugh too hard at these inflexible nectar philosophers, as a rigid ideology made fools of some German professors in this century. Only fifty years ago Nazi "biologists" rejected the simplicity of reciprocal evolution between flowers and insects. The thought that a butterfly benefited her food source merely by consistently carrying pollen on her legs seriously offended the Nazi vision of "Nature's Iron Law" in which superior "races" survived by dominating or destroying those weaker.

Scientists have sectioned flowers with sharp blades, stained the slices, and looked at them under the microscope. Nectaries are connected to the food-conducting veins (phloem) inside all flowering plants. Each nectary contains one or more strands of phloem or the nectary forms on top of a strand located below the glandular surface. Food made by green leaves is usually transferred to storage stems and roots by phloem. Flowers, though, have evolved from specialized leaves, so it's natural that they've retained some phloem over time and they can redirect the flow of food from green leaves into their nectaries.

We can see how watery foods are pumped into the nectary, but how do they escape to the surface? After all, flower skin is usually covered by a protective, transparent layer of wax and solid fats so nectaries start life wearing a coat of varnish. When the nectary hairs of a honeysuckle *(Lonicera)* start secreting the liquid, pressure of the nectar pushes off the waxy layer. In the flowers of some cacti, nectar escapes only after gland cells loosen up and disintegrate. Finally, some nectaries have holes punched in their waxy coats and these holes connect directly to wet pores in the gland tissue. Such nectary sieves are found in lemon and orange blossoms *(Citrus)*, for example.

The nectaries of closely related plants are almost always found on the same place inside their respective flowers. I've examined the flowers of species of wood sorrels *(Oxalis)* from North America and southern Africa. One knobby nectary is found at the base of *each* of the stalks (staminal filaments)

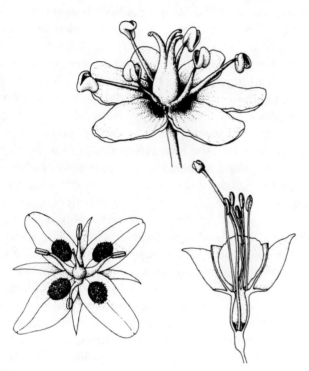

Nectar glands (blackened) are often found at the base of a flower's petals and/or sepals. *Above.* The death camas *(Zigadenus)* has a low pimply nectary on each of its six petallike organs.

Lower left. The green gentian *(Frasera)* has a large fringed nectary on each petal but none on its four narrow sepals.

Lower right. The petals and sepals of fuchsia *(Fuchsia)* form a bell-shaped tube with nectaries formed at the base of the tube. ILLUSTRATIONS BY W. W. DELANEY

that make up the outer ring of pollen-making stamens (see preceding chapter). In contrast, the flowers of all death camas species wear low, pimply nectaries at the base of each of the six, flat, petallike structures known as tepals.

A death camas nectary is also surrounded by a ring or splotch that's greenish-yellow in color. This is the nectar guide. The nectar guide does not make nectar but it advertises the location of the secretions to the pollinators. That's why so many flowers have sharply contrasting colors on their petals, freckles, or are stained with squiggly webs or lines that appear to trail off toward the base of the flower.

Some flowers take the location of nectaries to an extreme. They hide the gland at the base of long tubes or hollow spurs so the nectar is accessible only to animals with long tongues. The columbines in Chapter 12 are excellent examples of nectar concealed in spur tips. Nectar droplets do not always remain with the gland that secreted them. The sweet fluid may be drained off by channels and grooves cut into the flower's skin so it drips into deeper chambers or craters.

Even so, the placement of nectar in so many different flowers tells the same story over and over. The low position of a nectar pool forces thirsty animals to contact the sexual organs of the flower if they want to drink. The stamens sprinkle or brush the animal's head or body with pollen. When the animal enters a second flower, some of those pollen grains should adhere to the receptive tip of the pistil starting the next generation of seeds.

Honeybees have little hairy "spoons" at the tip of their long tongues so they lap up nectar the way a cat laps milk. They don't suck nectar (as the poets prefer). Some nectar will be used as a sort of "cement" to help keep pollen grains packed onto the pollen baskets on their hind legs. Most of the nectar, though, is stored in a gut sack and is taken back to the hive and shared. Honey, then, is what remains of flower nectar *after* the liquid has been "processed" by honeybees. Honey-

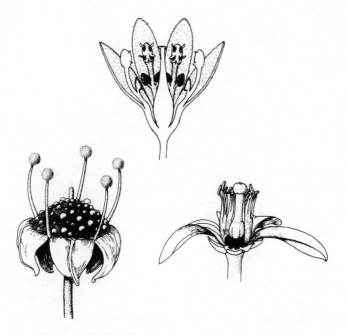

Nectaries may appear on other floral structures.
Above. The stamen stalks of avocado *(Persea)* wear nectar glands in pairs.
Lower left. The glandular "hump" in the center of the male flower of ivy
(Hedera) secretes droplets of nectar. *Lower right.* The pistil of the orange
blossom *(Citrus)* sits on a nectary shaped like a doughnut. ILLUSTRATIONS BY
W. W. DELANEY

bees usually do three things to nectar to convert it into the
honey we harvest from their combs. Two of these processes
occur inside the bee. First, big sugar molecules are broken
into smaller sugar molecules. That means most of the sucrose
in nectar is turned into its two component sugars: glucose and
fructose. Our own bodies do the same thing when we eat
white table sugar (yes, it's the same sucrose), but we digest the
sugars ourselves and don't share them with our sisters. Second, honeybees often add an enzyme to the nectar they pro-

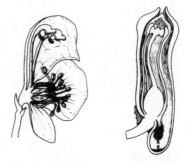

Some nectaries are well hidden, forcing foragers to search inside the flower. *Left.* The two petals of a monkshood's flower *(Aconitum)* end in nectary cups concealed *under* the sepal hood. *Right.* When the nectary of the fumitory *(Fumaria)* secretes, the fluid drips into a low petal sack. ILLUSTRATIONS BY W. W. DELANEY

cess. This enzyme should delay crystallization of the sugars, but cooking destroys this effect. If the honey in your pantry is getting crusty or has turned into amber rocks, the beekeeper probably subjected the comb to high heat to separate honey from beeswax. Stand the jar in hot water to melt the crystals.

The final stage of making honey is a group effort. The bee returns to her hive and regurgitates the contents of her honey sac. The droplet is passed to the jaws of a sister and this is repeated, "fireman's fashion," until the warmth of the hive evaporates the droplet down to the correct syrupy consistency before it goes into the comb.

It has been understood since the last century that the flowers of different species produce nectars with different sugar concentrations. That's why beekeepers must shift their hives to tap the richest sources as different crops, trees, or wildflowers come into bloom. You can measure the dissolved contents in flower nectar with a handy little device called a sugar refractometer. This piece of equipment can fit in a shirt pocket and is the same device used in hospitals and factories to test sugar levels in soft drinks and juice products.

The amount of sugar dissolved in a drop of nectar can vary with daily temperature, climate, the age of the flower, and water levels in the soil. After all, if the plant can't take up enough water through its roots, nectar production may stop or the usual proportions of sugar to water may collapse. I've taken nectar measurements of Australian plants during droughts and the nectar has almost caramelized in the floral cup.

The nectar of different flowers will give consistently different readings over the same season. The blooms on some American sagebrushes (*Salvia* spp.) secrete nectar with 25–45 percent dissolved sugars. Sugars in the nectar of morning glories (*Ipomea* spp.) hold around 30 percent. Sugar levels in my death camas nectar rarely went as high as 15 percent. This is rather pitiful and made me suspect the honeybees were really weak with hunger, not sick.

Of course, until a rather short time ago the scientific community did not have a very clear idea of what basic components were dissolved in nectar. The French botanist Gaston Bonnier attempted the first analysis of nectar sugars in 1878. Since then, about seven different sugar molecules have been positively identified, but most plant chemists never bothered to look for the unfamiliar. Nectar was regarded as a sweet tea (without cream).

A few chemists carried on and found that nectars contained small quantities of amino acids (the building blocks of proteins) and vitamin C. Real breakthroughs came in the early 1970s from a laboratory about half the size of a suburban kitchen, at the University of California at Berkeley. For almost twenty years evolutionary ecologist Herbert Baker and biochemist Irene Baker have continued to "scoop" botanical circles with news about nectar contents.

Herbert told me that the idea for breaking down each constituent in nectar came to him one evening while lying in a warm bathtub. His mind wandered over some papers he had

read about how some tropical butterflies feed on rotting car-
casses. Apparently, they must need something more substan-
tial than sugars. It made him wonder if "more conventional"
moths and butterflies obtained special nutrients from flower
nectars. The prospect fascinated his more practical wife. By
the time of Irene's unexpected and much lamented death,
only a few years ago, she had analyzed the nectars of hundreds
of flowering plants, from a crow-pollinated hibiscus of Hawaii
to a giant member of the pineapple family *(Puya)* from Chile.

Irene could keep a nectar library on her lab shelves because
it's so easy to store. Remove the nectar from the flower and let
the droplets dry on a spotlessly clean piece of filter paper. The
filter paper could be stored in a plastic sheet in a looseleaf
notebook until it was ready for treatment.

Yes, sugars were the dominant nutrients in nectar, but it
was amazing how many other compounds turned up in small
but consistent quantities. Nectar from a gland on the leaf of
the sunshine wattle (Chapter 9), for example, turned up
fifteen of the basic amino acids (from alanine to valine)
under Irene's analysis. Furthermore, nectar could contain its
own "nondairy creamers." This consisted of plant fats especially common in nectar from those flowers belonging to the
trumpet-vine family (Bignoniaceae). Nectars could be acidic
or alkaline. Following in the Bakers' wake, other researchers
would learn that the nectars of some flowers contained their
own enzymes and proteins.

After analyzing so many different flowers sharing similar
pollinators, the Bakers realized that there were predictable
patterns in nectar chemistry. Floral nectars seemed to fit the
dietary requirements and "life-styles" of the animals most
likely to transport pollen from flower to flower. If hummingbirds were the most important visitors, the flower usually
produced a sugar-rich nectar (high in sucrose) but very, very
low in amino acids. Hummingbirds are warm-blooded. The
energy they need comes largely from the sugars they burn off.

However, hummingbirds always supplement their diets with little insects they catch on the wing so they do not need nectar to provide "liquid meat."

In contrast, consider the case of those flowers pollinated by dung and carrion flies. Sugar concentrations are much lower and tend to be dominated by simple glucose and fructose. Flies are coldblooded and their levels of activity are dependent largely on the heat of the sun. The concentrations of amino acids in the nectar of such flowers are the highest known in nature. To keep bluebottles steady customers, the flower must offer a wet reward that simulates the "slushier aspects" of the manure heaps and rotting corpses in which such insects breed.

The death camas appears to secrete most of its nectar early in the morning after the dew on the grass has vanished but before it's warm enough for most insects to take flight. Nectar can be found on each tepal of each open flower. Each droplet resembles a transparent bead. I drew up these beads into glass capillary tubes finer than the quill of a canary's feather. Then I dotted pieces of filter paper with the fluid. When the nectar spots of the death camas dried I put the paper slips in cellophane bags, put the bags in an envelope, and mailed them off to Irene.

A reply arrived a few months letter. The nectar was free of any of the unusual sugars and rare amino acids known to sicken honeybees, but it had tested positive for the presence of alkaloids! The alkaloids are a huge class of plant compounds that can produce a fatal reaction in animal guts. Belladonna, strychnine, and caffeine are alkaloids, and you don't have to be Agatha Christie to know how they can harm people.

The death camas belongs to a small family of lilies (Melanthiaceae) with unusual powers. Juices from their underground stems or onionlike bulbs have been used to treat fever and hypertension. Commendable, but the death camas and its European allies have also been used as insecticides, poison baits for crows, and as ingredients in black magic. A sheep dies after eating a pound or two of death camas stalks. Research completed in the late fifties showed that honeybees died after eating death camas pollen. Forgive my ghoulish interest, but human beings, livestock, and honeybees may share some of the same signs of death camas poisoning: They *all* suffer from the staggers.

Death camas flowers now joined an elite but unrelated group of plants containing some unwholesome things in their nectar. It was quite a surprise to learn that some of the flowers with nectar testing positive for alkaloids included such garden regulars as pumpkin *(Cucurbita pepo)*, yellow flag iris *(Iris pseudocorus)*, and creeping bellflower *(Campanula rapunculoides)*. Of course, both honeybees and people are not harmed by all alkaloids. Still, it was a bit like learning that grandma had been spiking the chicken soup with arsenic for years.

There's no simple way to determine if nectar contains toxic principles based merely on the shape, color, or even the scent of a flower. No, Shakespeare's rhymed maxim at the end of Sonnet 94 won't work on a death camas:

> For sweetest things turn sourest by their deeds;
> Lilies that fester smell far worse than weeds.

Now, you needn't be frightened by the honey you buy at the supermarket or at a health-food shop. Most plants with alkaloid-rich roots or shoots produce the most harmless nectars. For example, the Bakers demonstrated that the nectar of tobacco flowers was free from any nicotine taint.

Considering the virulent range of poisons in the resins and leaves of so many tropical trees, countries like El Salvador and Brazil could never export their honey if jungle nectars were unsafe. My memory of wildflower honey in Central America is that it was the blandest stuff imaginable (like clover or apple blossom honey back home). The only unwholesome aspect was that the product was often sold to you in a dusty liquor bottle and "corked" with a dirty piece of dried corncob.

The real danger to man comes when the bees are unaffected by alkaloid nectars and pass far higher concentrations on to us as they evaporate that nectar to make honey. Of course, beekeeping is thousands of years old and we've learned to avoid placing our hives near flowers that are good for bees but bad for people. Written records of poisonous honey go back at least to 401 B.C. to the Persian campaign of the Greek commander Xenophon and his men, retreating from Asia Minor. On one occasion, the Greeks had had a good day beating their Colchian pursuers, but then they made the near-fatal error of raiding local villages for food by breaking open the peasants' hives. The people of that region allowed their honeybees to forage on the nectar of Pontic azalea *(Rhododendron luteum)*. It's believed the honey had pleasant narcotic qualities in *small* doses, but the Greeks were piggy. Here's Xenophon's version of what happened next:

> . . . all the soldiers who ate of the honeycombs lost their sense, and were seized with a vomiting and purging, none of them being able to stand upon their legs. Those who ate but little, were like men very drunk, and those who ate much, like madmen, and some like dying persons. In this condition great numbers lay upon the ground, as if there had been a defeat, and the sorrow was general. The next day, none of them died, but recovered their senses about the same hour they were seized; and the third and fourth day, they got up as if they had taken physic.

American beekeepers have had to learn the hard way that they must also keep their hives away from shrubs in the family Ericaceae, and that includes *our* native species of mountain

laurels *(Kalmia)*, rhododendrons, and azaleas. Over a century
ago a surgeon reported how the honey of mountain laurel
"overpowered" people.

The common thread in the reports of death camas poison-
ings is that people, livestock, and bees have suffered only
when they were very, very hungry and had virtually nothing
else to eat. That's certainly the case on the tallgrass prairie.
Over the seasons I've studied the death camas, I've found that
honeybees come for their toxic tea only in drought years
when preferred flowers like prairie turnip *(Psoralea esculenta)*
fail to bloom in the dry soils.

You may well ask, how does the death camas ever benefit
when its pollinator shuns it in good years and its flowers
murder honeybees in bad years? The answer is simple: Honeybees are *not* the true pollinators of the death camas. Honeybees are not the true pollinators of *any* plant native to North
America. Honeybees came to the New World as the servants
of European man, as did cows, horses, and sheep. So much
for the enthusiastic drive of a certain senator from Utah who
believes that the honeybee should become our national insect. That would be like replacing the bald eagle with the
chicken.

Spring after spring my death camas were pollinated by
native bees, a fraction of the size of the imported honeybee.
These short-tongued bees *(Dialictus)* visited the death camas
flowers taking nectar through good years and bad. About
three quarters of all the native bees collected on the death
camas carried the pollen of the death camas flower, to the
exclusion of every other prairie flower at Konza. That's certainly a good sign that the bees were immune to the death
camas poisons and depended on the flower's resources to
raise their larvae. I have hundreds of observations of these
little bees drinking death camas nectar but not a single record
of the same insects showing any of the symptoms of the des-
perate honeybees.

Have the *Dialictus* bees merely evolved some sort of detoxi-
fication program, or are they really deriving something special from death camas nectar—alkaloids and all? We still
don't know, but recent research by Keith Brown, at the Brazil-
ian University of Estadual de Campinas, has shown that some
adult butterflies search for the *nastiest* nectars. Obviously,
such insects have not read Tennyson:

> And most of all would I flee from the cruel madness of love—
> The honey of poison-flowers and all the measureless ill.

No, these hamadryad butterflies (ithomiids) drink the alkaloid nectars of tropical pyeweeds *(Eupatorium)*. If fresh pye-
weed flowers aren't available, they will raid dying borages and
heliotropes when their blossoms give up alkaloids as they rot.
Chemicals supped by the winged adults become concentrated
within their reproductive organs.

The butterfly's body makes new chemicals, based on the
nectar poisons. These new substances will be used to mark
territories, attract mates, and then some poisons are actually
transferred to their eggs making them distasteful to many
enemies. Considering the weird butterfly-pyeweed connection, a theory that *Dialictus* bees may protect their own children with a diet of death camas nectar and pollen can't be
dismissed yet.

One wonders how many wildflowers speckling Konza's hills
offer nectar too bitter for man or beast, but essential to some
insects? We may be using the wrong myth. Some nectars are
the gift of Hades, not Heaven. Throughout the world mother
insects may repeat the tale of Thetis dunking their Achilles'
eggs in the nectar of the Styx to ensure some measure of
invulnerability.

CHAPTER 8

The Hoon's Nest

hoon /hun/ *n. Colloq.* 1. a loutish, aggressive, or surly youth. 2. a fast, reckless driver. 3. a foolish or silly person, esp. one who is a show-off . . . -*v.i.* 5. to drive fast and recklessly.

The Macquarie Dictionary, second revision

. . . *hooligan*, bovver boy *(Brit. Colloq.)* disorderly person, goon, hellion, hoodlum, **hoon**, irresponsible, juvenile delinquent, larrikin, rugger-bugger, scourer *(Brit. Hist.)* . . .

The Macquarie Encyclopedic Thesaurus

If you were to rent a car in downtown Sydney and drive south toward Woolongong along the Prince's Highway, within an hour you'd be on the edge of Royal National Park. It's Australia's oldest national park, as its first piece of land was dedicated in 1879, so it's almost as old as Yellowstone in America. The park is so vast it encompasses most of the surviving environments isolated within the suburbanized, central coast of New South Wales. It would take me all day just to walk from the beach down into a rain-forest gully by crossing over heaths of *Banskia* and "hard leaf" woodlands of

Eucalyptus and wattle. Imagine how convenient such a varied, protected area is to a city-weary botanist like me, stuck "downtown" for most of the week.

If you had driven through Royal National Park within the last three years, you would have seen us working by the roadside. We must have presented an especially odd sight to the uninitiated on one October morning in particular. I was recording the number of open flowers on vines of the creeping guinea flower *(Hibbertia scandens)*. A technical officer from the Royal Botanic Garden caught native bees harvesting "guinea" pollen while our photographer took color slides of the pollinating insects. To make the situation more absurd we had all adopted the posture a scientist friend calls "the botanist's buns-up position." A number of passing cars slowed down and the occupants rubbernecked the four people crouching over the shrubbery with their lab-coated bottoms in the air.

After more than eight years of roadside research in the states of New South Wales, Victoria, and South Australia, I've become pretty oblivious to commuters' stares. If they stop and ask questions, I try to offer truthful and uncomplicated explanations. However, on a recent visit we experienced the uncomfortable feeling of angry eyes upon us. We noticed that a dilapidated van had stopped on the opposite side of the road. A meaty, sunburned face leaned out of the driver's window and treated us to a mean glare framed by long, greasy hair. We stared back, and his van took off with a screech of crunching gravel. What did we do to deserve his company? Well, after eight years in Australia, even I can identify a hoon. Everyone knows what hoons are up to out in the bush, but it seemed best to say nothing to my coworkers at the time.

Unfortunately, my worst suspicions were confirmed when I returned to the same site the following week with a curator and a new assistant. The assistant volunteered to explore the bush to find more flowering vines. Natasha returned ten minutes later announcing she'd located more creeping guinea flowers, and that "people are so predictable. You can't walk in a park these days without finding marijuana."

She had found two large, open cardboard boxes ineptly concealed among low bracken fern *(Pteridium esculentum)* and honeymyrtles *(Kunzea)*. Each box contained about six marijuana seedlings, and each plantlet had its own molded-folded flowerpot made of newspaper and cellophane. They had demonstrated how to make these cheap planters on *Gardening Australia* only a few weeks earlier. It's nice to know that even hoons take advantage of the educational programs offered by the national television station.

The three of us decided to live and let live. It didn't seem worth the effort to drive all the way back to the ranger's station to report such meager amounts of boo in the bush. In weeks to come, though, we learned we were not keeping a naughty secret. Once the rangers learned which site I had selected for fieldwork, they cautioned us to take extra care and record the licenses of "suspicious vehicles." It seems that my site had been under official observation for months!

We never saw our hoon again, but he left his calling card. The original boxes vanished before the end of October, only to be replaced in late December by a single box. By then, his efforts had gone upmarket. The paper jardinieres had been replaced by standard plastic pots. The remains of a bag of commercial soil mixture lay next to the box, giving it even greater visibility. "They're not going to survive," said Natasha. "He's not watering them."

In fact, the hoon couldn't have picked a worse place for his crop. Just beyond a pretty grove of Christmas bush *(Ceratopetalum gummiferum)* we found the remains of someone else's plantation of dreams. This time the authorities had been so determined to uproot all the evidence that they had literally cut out all the illegal plants using one or more turf roll-cutters. They had left such long, blank rectangles of bare earth with such sharp, precise corners, they resembled airstrips for model planes.

Before the police can charge anyone for growing marijuana in Australia, the plants must receive an official identification. It's quite likely that the goods confiscated at my site in Royal National Park turned up at the identification desk at the herbarium of the Royal Botanic Garden. Checking our *Cannabis* notebooks of the previous summer, the RBG identified over 2,037 plants from December through February (numbers have slumped over the years). Mind you, that's everything from leafing sprouts no longer than your pinky to robust adults over six feet high.

Sometimes the detectives don't want to drag these titans into the herbarium building and the botanist on duty has to look at a wilting heap in the back of the paddy wagon. Every New South Wales policeperson who brings in a marijuana plant will be given a special signed receipt of identification to use in conjunction with our specimen-examination forms.

The failed attempts of the accused to camouflage their illegal plants can be very funny. My favorite, last summer, had the stunted shoots of marijuana in fancy, hand-thrown pots (with fluted rims, no less), "companion planted" with philodendrons and oxalis in the hope of better concealment. The police compete with one another to see how many plants they can bring in at one time. One officer, a victim of the "companion planting" ruse, was distinctly disappointed when he learned that a few of the leaves he confiscated turned out to belong to a legal houseplant. He might have benefitted from a few lessons in plant taxonomy.

Trying to hide *Cannabis sativa* in wild reserves or parkland makes even less sense than trying to give it a sanctuary in the crazy quilt of most suburban gardens or greenhouses. After all, even the smallest gardens contain collections of plants from four or five continents. When plants from so many different parts of the globe are crammed together, the dif-

ferences between stem and leaf structures can blend or overlap. In contrast, marijuana is not native to the Australian
landscape and simply doesn't resemble any of the common
aspects of Australian vegetation in the temperate southeast.

Marijuana plants will always stick out in the bush, even
when the eye is not drawn to tilled earth or other signs of
cultivation. Each marijuana leaf is made up of three to seven
leaflets with "toothed" edges. They are arranged like fingers
on a hand, with the longest leaflets in the center. Living
Australian plants have *not*, by and large, adopted this type of
foliage, as it probably would have meant losing too much
water vapor in the dry air. Marijuana isn't even the right color
for the bush. Most of the native shrubs and taller herbs are
covered by such a thick, tinted layer of waxy fat that they have
a distinctive bluish-green cast absent on the leaves of marijuana.

Planting marijuana in a sunny spot a few yards off the
beaten track assumes incorrectly it will go undiscovered.
Rangers often patrol less accessible areas. There are always
visitors who wander off to answer the call of nature—or true
naturalists, like myself, who know they have to leave the path
to find the uncommon flora and fauna.

You can't hide *C. sativa* in deep shade and keep it profit-
able, either. The plant is a native of Central Asia, and ecologists suspect that marijuana displays all the characteristics of
an "r species." That means that the plant's short lifespan is
adapted to colonizing disturbed sites and channeling most of
its resources into the production of as many offspring as
possible. An r species can produce several generations in a
single season and its seeds sprout whenever soil, light, and
water conditions reach a temporary optimum. However, r
species are quickly evicted from open areas once the regener-
ation of spreading shrubs and taller trees overtake and out-
shade the bolting stems of marijuana.

Cannabis has been one of mankind's happiest "camp fol-

Above. Different hairs mix together on the surface of marijuana stems and leaves, but only hairs with rounded heads produce resin. Longer, hooked hairs make no resin but contain so much silica grit and calcium carbonate that they often survive burning. Criminologists may identify such hairs from ash samples! ILLUSTRATION BY W. W. DELANEY

Below. This developmental series of a resin hair shows how the structure starts as a dividing "foot cell" embedded in the outer skin. As the cells of the hair's head expand they secrete resin, pushing off their protective membrane. When the membrane ruptures, resin oozes out and the hair dies. ILLUSTRATION BY W. W. DELANEY

lowers," migrating to disrupted forests and prairies around the world as man broke up the soil with anything from a digging stick to a bulldozer. *Cannabis* seeds arrived in new regions not only as migrating weeds, but as treasured crops. The plants appear to have been in cultivation for at least eighty-five hundred years.

Some breeds of cattle are raised for meat and some for the quality of their milk. We prize some cultivars of apple for the taste of raw fruit, while other orchards specialize in apples used for cooking or cider. It's not surprising to learn that

there are two interrelated groups within *C. sativa* grown for
different purposes. Those plants that came from northerly
latitudes were grown for their stem fibers and for their seeds,
which yielded an oil similar in quality to that of linseed
(Linum). This breed of *Cannabis* is often called Indian hemp.
The arrival of this hemp *Cannabis* into Europe is so ancient it
seems to have been commemorated in Aesop's fable "The
Owl and the Birds." The birds have never seen hemp sprouting in a field before and see no threat. After the wise owl fails
to convince his fellows to devour this new seed, man converts
the hemp crop into the first snares and fowling nets.

On the other hand, the *Cannabis* of more southern regions
of Asia produced poorer fibers and lower quantities of seed
oil. Its stems and leaves had been selected for their potency in
folk cures and their powers of intoxication. The skin of all
Cannabis plants is clothed in little glands. The glands of the
southern crops tend to secrete the resins richest in a class of
pungent substances known as cannabinoid cannabinols.
These *Cannabis* plants are called marijuana, hashish, and
many other names (some unprintable).

Botanists often place *Cannabis* in the mulberry and fig
family (Moraceae). All of these plants have certain similarities
at both the tissue and organ levels—for example, the ducts
inside the plant that often produce a milky sap (latex). There
are two scales (stipules) flanking the sides of each leaf stalk.
The flowers are male or female and the ovary inside each
female flower should contain two seed-making chambers.
Cannabis has also been placed in its own family (Can-
nabaceae), which it shares only with the hopvines *(Humulus)*
once used so extensively to give beer its bitterness. The male
flowers of marijuana and hops have their organs arranged in
groups of five instead of the groups of four associated with
true fig and mulberry flowers.

The actual number of *Cannabis* species is a far more controversial problem and it may not be especially prudent of me to open what other authorities regard as an old wound. The passion with which some scientists have argued the merits of only one variable species versus three or more species has divided those scholars who study the roles of plants in different cultures (ethnobotany). Quarrels over the number of *Cannabis* species may have gone beyond the relative merits of using different methods and techniques for classification. It may have even gone beyond the changing philosophies of biologists asking that old but important question, Exactly what *is* a species?

The problem is that legal systems and scientific fact do not have much in common. The laws of most Western countries specifically forbid the possession of only one species of *Cannabis*, known as *C. sativa*. What happens, though, if a lawyer finds a witness willing to testify that the dried leaves found on the accused belong to something called *C. ruderalis* or *C. indica*? That's precisely what began to happen in the sixties and seventies when the drug culture became almost indistinguishable from the youth culture. Sympathy for young offenders is one thing, but is it good science?

Not according to Dr. Ernest Small, of the Biosystematics Research Institute in Ottawa, Canada, and the late Dr. Arthur Cronquist, of the New York Botanical Garden. They commented in their 1976 paper: "In the current *cause célèbre* some taxonomists who once published expressions of firm position that *Cannabis* comprises only one species, have sharply reversed themselves in testifying on behalf of defendants charged in narcotics cases."

Small and Cronquist had a long, hard look at the history of *Cannabis* classification. They compared collections of both dried and living plants, counted and measured chromosomes, experimented on the breeding behavior when different plants were grown together, and even contrasted resin chemistry. In short, they completed all the usual tasks of botanists who are expected to use the evidence to make some sort of systematic interpretation.

They came to the conclusion that there remained only one variable species, *C. sativa.* You could break the one species into two subspecies if you wanted to, but why bother? The two subspecies regularly crossed with each other without any ill effects to their offspring. Weedy forms crossed with hemp crops and vice versa. Any real differences remained almost purely chemical. Subspecies *sativa* was grown for oil and fibers, so many cannabinoids were either absent or weakly represented. Subspecies *indica* was consistent in having the most potent resin. Any differences in plant anatomy, a more reliable indicator for identifying separate species, could not be distinguished readily.

There seems to be some consensus among the majority of plant taxonomists favoring Small and Cronquist's treatment of *Cannabis.* The matter must remain unresolved, though, since different botanists often place different emphases on the range of characters used to describe each species. The identification of plants in a cardboard box is rather unrelated to my research. No, my task is more related to ecology than taxonomy.

Every time a tree falls in an Australian forest some native shrubs and herbs are so stimulated by the excess sunlight reaching the forest floor that they produce massive populations until new trees shoot up, spread their branches, and plug up the break. Once this occurs, the smaller plants retreat into long periods of dormancy or actually die back. That's why I prefer to work in those Australian environments that have received minor disturbance either by man, cyclical fires, storms, or the usual rates of tree senility. Interrupt the canopy to put in a highway and you may end up with some of the richest, densest populations of wattles, discussed in Chapter

9, and the ground-dwelling orchids of Chapter 14. Light gaps also appear to benefit many species of mistletoes, parrot peas, and the guinea flowers that currently hold my attention. The same disturbances also serve the immediate needs of those who plant marijuana.

Don't ask me to take sides. Until the state and federal governments effect a solution satisfying to all, the Australian bush will deteriorate at two levels. First, the cycle of hoons breaking up the earth to plant pot, and police razing the plantations, will mean that many habitats will never be able to regenerate. The forest at my site in Royal National Park has been gradually closing in on a space where a farm once stood. The coarser ferns and sedges spread into the abandoned pastures, forming a cradle encouraging the establishment of shorter shrubs and creeping vines. Given sufficient time, the layer of shrubs and vines would have yielded to invasions of eucalypt seedlings spread by the encroaching forest. The original habitat will never be restored while destructive skirmishes result in uprooting every native plant from a piece of soil.

Second, the bush becomes a less secure place for us all with marijuana's status as an illegal luxury item. No national parks were planned offering space and facilities for people in either drug production or prevention. Both pensioners and people living "alternative life-styles" in wooded areas around towns like Nimbin have complained of harassment by hoons and subsequent disruptions when local law enforcement is replaced by federal agencies. Neither cares which side shoots them first.

Every botanist who chooses to do fieldwork knows that an expedition to unfamiliar areas will involve collecting specimens, recording your observations, and dealing with the unexpected. Had I lived in another century, an expedition could have proved fatal due to disease, animals, or accidents along the trail. Historically, far finer botanists than I have succumbed. Despite the danger posed by hoons, it is a lot safer to be a part of botanical exploration as we approach the end of the twentieth century.

Regular vaccinations and antimalarial drugs protected me from the worst microbes while I was in the tropical Americas. My encounters with "dangerous beasts" can be summed as coming a little too close to three poisonous snakes over seventeen years (only one attempted to lunge at me). As for accidents along the trail, so far I've avoided the discomforts experienced by a coworker who has driven his jeep off mountain and volcanic slopes more than once.

Truthfully, the only time I've ever felt seriously threatened is when I've come across members of my own species in the field. In Central American countries, landowners employ vigilantes who patrol forest paths for poachers and woodcutters. I met these men on four separate occasions in El Salvador and Guatemala, without mishap. The first few moments of being approached by heavily armed gentlemen, *always* on horseback, are harrowing. Invariably, though, they turned out to be courteous upon discovering that they had met a real *profesor de botánica*. They also proved helpful sources of information regarding the common names and folk remedies of species under their protection.

Then there was the severe woman accompanied by her chauffeur/guard who pounced on us as we were emerging from an old Salvadoran lava flow known as El Pedregal de San Isidro. She claimed she owned the property (inherited from her late husband) and demanded to know what we were doing there! Once again my academic standing pacified the locals. I thought nothing more of it until I repeated the story to the ladies with whom I was boarding. They were horrified. Didn't I know that this woman had laid a false claim to that property? She had killed her employer/lover (not her husband) to gain the land, and it was reported that she was using El Pedregal as a dumping ground for the bodies of troublesome workers.

We returned to the same land without incident and I still discount most of the original gossip.

You don't expect such incidents in a First World country like Australia. The prospect of running into more members of the drug war does put an uncomfortable dimension on organizing an expedition. This is not to imply that Americans should feel altogether safe in their own woodlands. While botanizing in North Carolina in the seventies we were warned against visiting certain areas, although they were public land. The preparation of moonshine is still a jealously guarded "industry" in certain parts of the American South. Furthermore, a recent letter from the Missouri Botanical Garden warned that it's much too dangerous for scientists and tourists to visit some of the last native forests in the mountains of Hawaii, as their marijuana growers are armed. Whose forest is it anyway?

Natasha was right about our hoon's irregular care of his crop. We revisited the same site in Royal National Park last March. The same box was there but every potted plantlet was crispy dead. Had our presence chased away the hoon? As my dear grandmother would have said, "Don't touch the nest or the mother will never come back."

PART FOUR

In Pursuit of the Beautiful

CHAPTER 9

Wattles for the Empress

> We'll make the tyrants feel the sting
> Of those that they would throttle;
> They needn't say the fault is ours
> If blood should stain the wattle.
>
> Henry Lawson, "Freedom on the Wallaby"

When you live in southern Australia, it's easy to succumb to an annual craving that hits you during the last month of winter (August) on through mid-spring (October). Once the weekend arrives you are ready to pack your car with a picnic lunch, tea service, an "esky" filled with beer, and any sundry friends or relatives. You drive off to your favorite stretch of bushland and look for gold. It's wattle season and the gold you're searching for is the floral gold of blossoms worn by the trees and shrubs of the genus *Acacia*.

The sight of *Acacia* in bloom is breathtaking. It's almost as if the bluish-green foliage has been cloaked in a rich, yellow fleece. During wattle season this saffron mantle can be found from the southern coasts to the inland deserts, since the *Acacia* species have conquered most of the island continent. The cheerful colors of wattle blooms are so omnipresent that, until the turn of this century, both naturalists and "bush

poets" often referred to the spring as the maiden with yellow
hair. Isn't it ironic that Australians enjoy the spring gold of
wattle blossoms during the same months in which Americans
haunt their freeways in search of the gold of autumn leaves?

Wattle remains the most common name Australians give to
their seven hundred to nine hundred *Acacia* species, and
some botanists insist that the continent will yield over twelve
hundred species, once the great northwestern section is properly explored. The name *wattle* stems from the early days of
colonization. Settlers once cut the slender branches of many
different varieties of native shrubs and small trees, then
bound them together to form wattling, or covered them with
mud to make wattle and daub walls and fences. Today,
though, *wattle* is a word that is so closely associated with *Acacia*
species that the average Australian may not know that previous generations called the same plants myall, brigalow, umbrella bush, yarran, native hickory, miljee, and dead finish!

Australians do remain "bound" to their wattles by strong
sentiments, since the shrubs recall pioneer days. Wattle designs decorate such everyday items as mugs, tablecloths, tea
towels, greeting cards, the covers of poetry books, and illustrations in children's stories. There was the Wattle Club to honor
women who played cricket for Australia and the Wattle Blossom League for ladies to promote patriotic feelings for Australia.

This century has seen several unsuccessful attempts by citi-
zens to organize a national Wattle Day (a sort of Arbor Day
for native plants, especially acacias) for the first of September.
These efforts seem doomed to failure. Australia is such a vast
and variable continent that the flowering season of only one
wattle species, distributed through several different states and
climatic zones, may vary by more than a month. Therefore,
how can anyone find a single day that best coincides with the
flowering peaks of hundreds of different species?

In August 1988 the golden wattle *(Acacia pycnantha)* be-

A ti tree flower *(Leptospermum spectabile)* shows nectar oozing from a green gland lining the center of the flower and surrounding the neck of the pistil. PHOTO BY JAIME PLAZA

Above. To reach the nectar in the shallow cup of a white-flowered ti tree *(L. flavescens)* the jewel beetle *(Stigmodera)* must push aside the flower's stamens barring the way. PHOTO BY TREVOR HAWKESWOOD

Below. The cyclamen-flowered narcissus *(N. cyclamineus)* is a true daffodil. Each stalk ends in a single flower, and each flower has a corona that is longer than it is wide. PHOTO BY P. E. BRANDHAM

came the national floral emblem of Australia by official commonwealth proclamation made by the governor-general, Sir Ninian Martin Stephen (just in time for the bicentennial). "If blood should stain the wattle" is a phrase that dates back to rural uprisings during the depression of the 1890s. It is still used in some labor circles to warn both management and government to think twice about settling any industrial dispute with a heavy hand.

The British often think that their Australian cousins are extremely funny when they devote themselves to shrubs with such an ugly name. Back in the seventies, the Monty Python troupe could always raise a laugh by affecting bad Australian accents, holding beer cans up in the gesture of a toast, and reciting their version of the Australian National Anthem. How did it go? "This is the wattle / The symbol of your land / You can put it in a bottle / You can hold it in your hand." Mocking colonials is never a good idea, in retrospect. Wattles have complex roles within antipodal environments. Furthermore, we will see that they were treasured by royalty long before they held the public's affection.

What accounts for the sheer density and diversity of Australian wattles? In fact, you can't pin the plasticity of *Acacia* on any single adaptation. These large, woody plants are surprisingly adept at hiding the many secrets of their survival. Serious investigators must be prepared to employ a range of tools from shovels to electron microscopes.

Botanists insist that the number of *Acacia* species in Australia will eventually be double that of the known *Eucalyptus* species (the ubiquitous gum trees, ironbarks, bloodwoods, and mallees). Wattles encroach where eucalypts "fear to sprout." While tall eucalypt forests dominate the moist countryside around the coasts, wattles seem most successful in the dry "dead heart" that covers two thirds of the continent. Wattles recover rapidly from long droughts and tolerate poor soils. The secret lies in their roots, which are covered with swollen knobs. Like those of clover *(Trifolium)*, and other members of the pea and bean family, such root nodules are really living condominiums packed with microbes that fix nitrogen compounds. Since these microorganisms share their nitrogen with their wattle landlords, these shrubs and trees have repeatedly colonized some of Australia's most depleted regions. A few *Acacia* species have even been declared "noxious weeds" as they encroach on pasturelands and outcompete European grasses for their share of the low rainfall. Some of these wattles have even developed poisonous strains that accumulate fluorine compounds toxic to browsing sheep and cattle.

Things become even more interesting when you examine the plant above the soil surface. The shrubs may look quite lush, but the vast majority of Aussie wattles lack true leaves at maturity. The tough, fibrous green foliage is really a mass of flattened branches known as phyllodes. The wattle seedling will bear a few soft, feathery leaves after it sprouts, but these true leaves are usually replaced by the durable phyllodes as the plantlet grows taller and sturdier. A phyllode can do everything a leaf can do in the photosynthetic department, but it seems more resistant to the punishment of drying heat and the attacks of insects and marsupials.

Wattle blossoms also trick the eye. Each pom-pom or fuzzy sausage is really a mass of smaller flowers. More than thirty individual "florets" may be compressed into a single blossom head or spike. Each floret, in turn, bears five petals, but they are so reduced and scalelike that they are often invisible to the human eye. The brilliant displays we appreciate are due almost entirely to the way the pollen-filled stamens are massed together. Stamens may be tinted from a pearly off-white to canary yellow to deep orange. Spectacular shows are assured, since a single floret may bear more than a hundred individual stamens (depending on the species). Considering the hun-

Some wattle seedlings produce three different kinds of foliage within a couple of months. A base pair of simple seed leaves (cotyledons) are the first to emerge from the new shoot. They are replaced quickly by feathery compound leaves, which then give way to flattened, tough green branches, or phyllodes, in most Australian species. ILLUSTRATION BY W. W. DELANEY

dreds of thousands of florets produced by the branches of some trees and shrubs, the sheer calculation of the minutiae of wattle gold remains staggering.

Wattle stamens do more than make color and pollen, though. They have wrinkled tips that contain supplies of essential and volatile oils. The scent of a wattle grove on a warm spring day can be intense, although scents vary with species and temperature. Hedge wattles *(A. paradoxa)* smell like a combination of ripe pears and honey. The wirilda *(A. retinodes)* has a cloying odor as if someone spilled a commercial toilet water over a bowl of ripe melon balls.

The oddest feature of Australian wattles is best appreciated under the microscope. Most plants release their pollen as loose, separate grains. Wattle pollen is always fused together into flat, circular clusters known as polyads. Wattle polyads always have fused grains in multiples of four. It is common, for example, to find species of Australian wattles that arrange

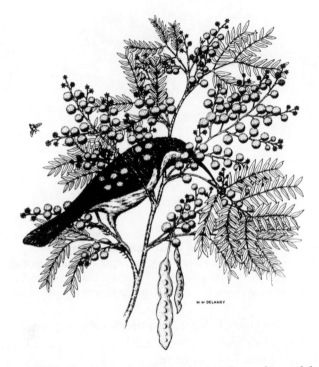

Sunshine wattle keeps its feathery leaves as an adult tree, but each leaf stalk develops a large red gland offering nectar while the plant blooms in autumn. Songbirds like this eastern spinebill *(Acanthorhynchus tenuirostris)* carry pollen from tree to tree because the bird is "powdered" by the open pom-poms while drinking nectar. ILLUSTRATION BY W. W. DELANEY

eight, twelve, or sixteen grains per polyad. Under the microscope these polyads look uncannily like pans of hot cross buns.

Only a few years ago many botanists believed that polyads were adapted for wind pollination. Spring breezes were thought to catch each polyad and send it spinning through the air like a Frisbee until it landed on the receptive tip of a wattle pistil. Most recent research has dispelled this "flying saucer" theory of pollination. Flies and tiny bees are attracted

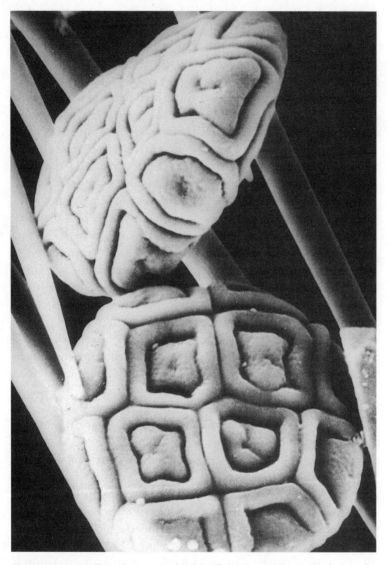

Here are two pollen clusters (polyads) of *Acacia* caught in the hairs of a bee's leg. Each cluster is made of sixteen grains (the four grains in the center have four more grains behind them). PHOTO BY PETER BERNHARDT

to wattle blossoms due to their bright colors and agreeable perfumes. Collecting polyads requires little effort on the part of a native bee. There are so many stamens to choose from, and eight polyads are arranged in slots at the swollen tip of each stamen like waffles popping up in a toaster. The bluish, crimson, and black bees look quite striking when they wear billowing masses of yellow polyads on their legs. Cross-pollination occurs as these insects fly from bush to bush.

Even native songbirds like the silvereyes *(Zosterops)*, thornbills *(Acanthiza)*, and spinebills *(Acanthorhynchus)* may become involved in cross-pollination. Individual florets of wattle appear to be too small and compressed to have functional nectar glands. However, the leaves or phyllodes of a few species, like the sunshine wattle *(A. terminalis)*, bear large red glands that brim with sugar and amino acid solutions each morning, while the small trees remain in flower in late summer through autumn. As the birds search each branch for drinks they are "powdered" by overhanging blossoms, and polyads cling to their head and breast plumage (most probably by static electricity). These migratory and nomadic birds may be more efficient "long-distance" pollinators than little bees.

Let me emphasize that functional nectar glands on wattle foliage is extremely common, although most species bear small glands instead of large red troughs. Nectar droplets on phyllodes may confer two advantages in a wattle life-cycle. First, as mentioned above, they may feed pollinators like bees and birds.

Second, this nectar also attracts a number of aggressive insects, especially ants. The ants protect their food source from munchers like caterpillars and beetles. When ants find a food source they may defend it from all other insects disrupting wattle eaters. Ecologist Andrew Beattie has taken me on wattle walks through the Australian bush and has shown me how different ants glean the nectaries at different times of the day and night. There are more ant species in Australia than on any other continent. The size and temperament of the "ant mafia" can be dazzling and aggressive.

I remember one violent murder on the phyllodes of a golden wattle. It was nearly one P.M. and the phyllodes were patrolled by ponerine ants known as skipjacks. Skippies have excellent vision, for ants, and are armed with scissorlike mandibles on one end and a cruel sting on the other. They like wattle nectar but are often regarded as meat eaters.

One skipjack, about as long as my thumbnail (rather small for a ponerine), found a green caterpillar chewing on a phyllode. The caterpillar attempted to "hide" from the ant by holding itself erect and masquerading as a twig. It didn't work. The sickle jaws of the ant clamped around the victim's waist. Then it rammed its stinger into the soft body of the caterpillar at least three times with sharp, directed thrusts. The caterpillar squirmed for a moment, then went limp, and the skipjack yanked it off the phyllode with a twisting motion and hauled the corpse back to its nest.

Another conceivable benefit of ant protection may have something to do with the time lag in pod growth. Some wattle species may wait more than six months for a fertilized pistil to become a mature, seed-filled pod. Ants may protect the young seeds from parasitic beetle larvae or any number of other, larger creatures that find wattle embryos tasty and nutritious.

Mature wattle pods split open, but each of the seeds may continue to dangle from the dried halves of the pod wall by means of a connective stalk known as the funiculus. Seed stalks that are long and wide, odorless, and bright red or yellow tend to be gathered by birds. Native pigeons and doves may swallow both seed and connective stalk, but they usually regurgitate the hard seed unharmed. Smaller, perching birds simply peck away at the stalk flesh, and the seed drops safely to the ground to be gradually covered by twigs, leaves, and shifting soils.

Other wattles display seeds with stubby, whitish-ivory stalks. These seeds often fall to the ground as the dry pods curl and twist. These stalks have a pleasing "nutty" smell, and the oily flesh tastes a bit like almond or walnut meats. Such seeds are gathered by large numbers of harvester ants. The ants carry the seeds down into their burrows and eat the oily stalks. The hard seeds are normally discarded in underground "trash pits."

The aboriginals, or native peoples of Australia, also respected wattle as a food source. They did not discriminate between seed and seed stalk, though. Women collected seeds and seed stalks, pounding the contents into oily cakes. These cakes have been analyzed and the levels of protein and carbohydrates they contain rival those found in the soybean. When wattle stems are injured they may exude an aromatic gum that the aboriginals used to make a sort of candy by soaking it in water with the honey of wild bees.

Of course, when the Dutch, French, and British explored the Australian continent they were not looking for exotic confections. They did, however, recognize unusual and beautiful plants. Most wattles arrived in Europe as dried specimens, but the great voyages had gardeners and botanists on their exploration teams, so every attempt was made to bring exotics back alive. Alien greenery became the possession of the Georges, Bonapartes, and Hapsburgs. For example, twenty-six species of wattles were growing at Kew Gardens by 1813, but most had arrived as seeds collected by Sir Joseph Banks during Captain Cook's voyage to the Pacific before 1780.

A royal plant needs a professional portrait. The first live Australian wattle to receive the official treatment was the sunshine wattle *(A. terminalis)*, around 1800. The flowering branch came from a Parisian garden and was painted by Henri Joseph Redouté (brother of the royal rose portraitist). The French have continued to cherish acacias, as both Asian and Australian species form the basis of the "mimosa" industry at Grasse. Australian botanists have returned from Grasse stunned at having seen so many groves of black wattle *(A. decurrens)* and silver wattle *(A. dealbata)*. Their blossoms remain popular as cut flowers, and their essential oils are used in such diverse products as perfumes, scented soaps, and even hair restorers!

Joséphine Bonaparte may have been the greatest patron of the wattle. Part of her estate of Malmaison was an Australian garden complete with black swans sailing on the lake and small wallabies bouncing on the lawn. I've seen some of the old drawings and it looks like wattles (probably *A. terminalis*) grew among the shrubbery. The empress's achievements in horticulture were respected as much as her husband's rapacity was feared. Despite the Napoleonic wars, an order from the British Admiralty went out to its fleet, "that should any enemy prize captured on the high seas contain plants or seed addressed to the Empress, their safe and speedy passage was to be assured."

Later monarchs have been presented with artificial but expensive wattles. When the young Queen Elizabeth visited Australia in 1954, the government presented her with a floral brooch. The wattle "blossoms" were made of yellow diamonds.

If Australian wattles enjoyed such a grand sponsorship, why aren't they more common in cultivation in the Northern Hemisphere? The early horticulturists found them almost impossible to strike from cuttings. That left starting from seeds, but results were unpredictable. Most of the Australian plants required warm shelters through freezing winters. As botanical expeditions to the Far East progressed, the culture of Australian plants declined, in general. Wattles were passed

This 1824 vignette from an atlas of the Baudin Expedition to the antipodes depicts the Australian section of Joséphine Bonaparte's garden, complete with appropriate pets like "pygmy" emus (now extinct), black swans, and wallabies. The spindly tree with the feathery leaves *(left from center)* is probably sunshine wattle *(A. terminalis)*. F. PERON AND L. FREYCINET (FROM THE COLLECTION OF S. DUCKER)

over for the hardier lilies, peonies, rhododendrons, and magnolias from China or Japan, as we will see in Chapter 11.

Europeans did not know that wattle seeds covered by shifting sands or neatly tossed into a burrow wait for cyclical bushfires. Such seeds rarely germinate after winter rains, as they are well sealed inside their thick shells. The natural weak point on this shell is a special scar known as the hilum. The hilum is the seed's "belly button," because it marks where the seed was attached to the inside of the ovary wall by means of its fleshy stalk.

A wattle seed needs the temperature of the earth to increase sharply but briefly, so that its seed scar blisters and pops exposing the embryo to air and water. Bushfires kill many adult wattles, but a quick, fierce burn in late summer or early autumn stimulates the seed bank hidden in the insulating soil. After the winter rains come, the scorched ground may be clothed in the feathery leaves of sprouting wattles.

Remove wattle seeds from the "burn and bust open" cycle of Australian woodlands and you may still have one of the most patient life forms on this planet. The black coat sealing the embryo is so durable a form of packaging it should be envied by the food industry.

In 1991 Ms. Wendy Lowe of Cremorne, New South Wales, found a bag of seeds in her great-grandfather's desk drawer. He had been headmaster of a country school and he encouraged his students to cultivate native plants. Ms. Lowe cut off the red tape binding the packet but saved the old label which read, "Arbor Day, 1890." She planted the seeds of golden wattle and they sprouted into healthy plantlets (now on display at the Mt. Annan Botanic Garden, outside Sydney).

Joseph H. Maiden, the great Australian botanist, understood the survival mechanisms of wattle seeds a century ago. He also wanted schoolchildren to help brighten up gardens and roadsides with native wattles (it's possible he sent Ms. Lowe's ancestor the original bag). Maiden suggested soaking wattle seeds in near-boiling water. This is a perfectly effective technique, but modern botanists have their own tricks, which give germination a "kinky" touch. One coworker touches each seed with the lit end of her cigarette. Some physiologists prefer to place the seeds in the microwave oven for ten seconds or less.

Quick, clean methods of sprouting seeds and caring for the plantlets have encouraged many Australians to add both rarer species and new hybrids to their gardens. Australian wattles have begun to colonize the United States, although they seem most confined to southern California. The freeways leading out of Los Angeles now remind me and my wife of the planted landscapes around Melbourne. Some of the gardens at the larger universities, such as Berkeley, almost mirror sections of the Royal Botanic Garden in Sydney.

Unfortunately, identifying the common garden wattle in Europe or America remains a baffling task for a formally trained botanist. Plants marketed under the name of a good species often fail to resemble their wild ancestors. Plant breeders have selected for spectacular flowering features by searching both wild populations and commercial nurseries for bizarre mutations. The great gardens of Europe often neglected to notice spontaneous hybrids affected by the foraging honeybees. Offspring of these clandestine unions have been released to the public over many decades.

For those who prefer their wattles *au naturel,* the wildflower industry has become big business for Australian tourism. In western Australia, entire trains may be chartered to better appreciate wattles and other flowering plants in the land-scape. Not even the Empress Joséphine ever enjoyed the luxury of such an easy day trip.

....

CHAPTER 10

White Nun/
Yellow Nymph

Yesterday I cut an orchid, for my buttonhole. . . . In a thoughtless moment I asked one of the gardeners what it was called. He told me it was a fine specimen of *Robinsoniana,* or something dreadful of that kind. It is a sad truth, but we have lost the faculty of giving lovely names to things. Names are everything.

Oscar Wilde, *The Picture of Dorian Gray*

What's in a scientific name? Every time a new species is discovered and described, it receives a double-word name (its genus and species) to serve as its identity card in any future publication. This procedure has the international approval of the modern scientific community and it has been used for over two hundred and thirty years on everything from slime molds to seagulls. At a very basic level you should be able to break down the Greek or Latin syllables in each name and learn a little bit about the organism's anatomy, or color, or habits, or distribution. More often, you learn something about the individual who thought up the name and wrote the technical description.

Let's take the work of John Lindley (1799–1865), for example, as his names for orchids are particularly revealing. So many of his Greek names describe the shapes of leaves and branching stems, or point out minute sculptures on and in the petals and sexual organs. We know that Lindley was an enthusiastic and meticulous botanist who used living material and pickled flowers when available, since the succulent parts of orchids are often obscured or ruined by pressing and drying. Other species have been named after aristocratic orchid growers, botanical artists, and individuals who brought back the plant from exotic and dangerous places. Lindley was a courteous man and a diplomat for his discipline. He understood that the discovery and nurture of a new plant was a communal effort that extended far beyond the efforts of an individual stocking his museum cabinet.

There are moments, though, when you have the feeling that Lindley was so bewitched by some plants he was only comfortable consulting the great poets or the classic historians. Tiny flowers with bizarre shapes were named after the king of the elves *(Oberonia)* and a Greek vampire that assumed animal forms *(Empusa)*. Beautiful flowers could be approached almost playfully, as he reminds us of the goddess of mischief in the genus *Ate* and the classical "nicknames" for Venus *(Doritis)* and Helen of Troy *(Lacaena)*. Both the virtuous and the lustful are commemorated in a vestal virgin *(Laelia)* and a courtesan who took the fancy of Pericles *(Aspasia)*.

Lindley erected the genus *Lycaste* in 1843 so future botanists would discriminate between some species with large, showy flowers and pleated leaves from their cousins, the parrakeet-tongue orchids *(Maxillaria)*. *Lycaste* was named for the daughter of Priam, Troy's last king. According to one version of the myth, Lycaste escaped the wretched fate of her parents and siblings when the gods took pity on her and changed her into a sea nymph. One modern grower of *Lycaste* orchids insists they were named after Helen of Troy's sister. Surely, though, Helen's only sister was the vengeful Queen Clytemnestra.

Lycaste was introduced to British and European glasshouse

culture just as the nineteenth-century passion for orchids entered its second, and most enduring, peak of popularity. Collectors demanded novelty, and they were most charmed by one *Lycaste* species, in particular, because it could produce pure-white blossoms. This species is properly known as *Lycaste skinneri* after its British collector, George Skinner. By 1867 orchid writers like James Bateman recognized it as "a universal favorite." However, more growers and naturalists have known this species as *L. virginalis*. When two or more scientists give the same plant different names accidentally, the oldest description should take precedence (*skinneri* appeared in print in Britain two years before *virginalis* in France). Guess which name is preferred, though? Oscar Wilde was right. Names *are* everything!

Honor and patriotic glory have been heaped on *L. skinneri*, which is distributed naturally through southern Mexico and Central America. It is the national flower of Guatemala, and in 1939 its portrait was presented, for the first time, on a two-centavo stamp. More expensive stamps have followed. It is the symbol of the Guatemalan Orchid Society.

In my opinion, though, the most impressive thing about this species is that it is one of the few wild orchids which has a common name in Latin America. Orchids are such common wildflowers through Central America that Spanish-speaking peasants call all of them *conchitas* (little shells) or just *parasitas* (parasites, after their habit of clinging to tree branches). Almost every Guatemalan, Salvadoran, or Honduran knows *L. skinneri* as *la monja blanca* (the white nun), since the configuration of the floral organs is reminiscent of the old-fashioned nun's habit. The flowers are so closely associated with whiteness and purity that a bottled mayonnaise has been marketed under the name Monja Blanca through Central America. I remember that the contents of the jar never tasted as good as the flower looked.

The color of *L. virginalis* petals varies, and pure whites

aren't all that common in nature. There are white nuns, pink nuns, and violet nuns. The three petals on each flower are usually decorated with rosy to royal-purple splotches and lines. Horticulturalists may break these forms into definitive varieties with grand-sounding names like *delicatissima, picturata, purpurata,* and *alba* (for the pure white), but most scientists don't think such tints have much significance in classification. There are a few other *Lycaste* species that may produce white petals, like *L. deppei* and *L. macrophylla.* The majority of species offer floral parts ranging from polished yellow into rich orange and even shades of apple green, reddish brown, and chocolate. One wonders if a sea nymph, composed of foam and ivory, would have been considered an appropriate name model had Lindley been on more familiar terms with these duskier beauties.

These more richly colored species would also find a most appreciative audience. Their floral organs tend to be stiff, oval, and often point upward. Growers have enjoyed displaying them on low benches or at ground level as if they were a sort of Hispanic tulip. Like so many tropical orchids discussed in Chapter 1, some lycastes' blossoms may live more than a month.

Lycaste orchids are exclusive to the tropical Americas. A few are scattered through the West Indies, but the majority occur from the Yucatán peninsula down to southern Bolivia. Older books list as many as forty species, but more recent publications have kept the numbers down to twenty-five to thirty. Most *Lycaste* species seem to prefer life in those forests covering misty mountains; they become most common between two to four thousand feet above sea level. Their flowering may be cued by cyclical patterns of weeks of cool, dry nights.

This pattern of finding the greatest number of *Lycaste* species on mountain slopes that "corral the clouds" is repeated by the majority of orchid genera throughout the New World tropics. Let that be a lesson to you if you want to go orchid-

The flowers of wild plants of the white nun, *Lycaste skinneri (virginalis)*, may show as many as eight different color patterns, and such patterns have been treated as natural varieties. Three color patterns have been drawn on the same plant for convenience. *Left.* Lip petal white with lateral petals purplish *(purpurea); middle,* lip petal deep purple with lateral petals white *(purpurata); right,* lip petal speckled *(vestalis).* ILLUSTRATION BY W. W. DELANEY

watching the Mexican or South American way. Stay out of lowland rain forests. The high temperatures, poor air movement, and soggy conditions cause disease and root rot in most orchids.

You don't find lycastes growing in forest soils much. In most species the ripe, dry capsule splits open months after fertilization and thousands of microscopic seeds drift away on the breeze. The most fortunate ones land on the wrinkled bark of a tree limb or, perhaps, in a tiny fissure of a volcanic boulder, and they hang on with ropey, adhesive roots as adults. In Izabal, Guatemala, *L. bradeorum* colonized the crumbling walls of Mayan ruins. Members of orchid expeditions must have been in for some nasty shocks when they attempted to pull lycastes off trees or boulders, as the spiny plants of *L. macrobulbon* seem to be a favorite hiding place of pit vipers. My own first encounter with lycastes was far more benign but no less wondrous.

The Tourist Center of Cerro Verde (Spanish for Green Hill) is located on top of a two-thousand-meter-high mountain in El Salvador. It boasts a fine hotel known throughout Central America for its gardens that mix native plants with fancy topiary and aromatic groundcovers. The government of the Republic of El Salvador completed the center during the late 1950s to overlook the then still active cone of the Izalco volcano, the former "lighthouse of the Pacific." Izalco petulantly sputtered out almost thirty years ago, spoiling the unique opportunity to dance by the light of a volcano in the hotel's dining room. The hotel had to offer new diversions to attract potential patrons. Izalco's now infrequent wisps of smoke, while sinister, had lost much of their drawing power.

Nearly twenty years ago the gardeners completed an orchidarium that contained a fine representative collection of orchid species found in the remaining mist forest below the hotel and from the adjoining slopes of the Santa Anna volcano. When I entered the orchidarium, in February, six pots

Most lycastes pass their lives clinging to boulders or branches. Yellow nymphs like *L. cruenta* often flower only after they shed their seasonal leaves exposing the nasty spines tipping each pseudobulb. ILLUSTRATION BY W. W. DELANEY

of *L. cruenta* greeted me with profuse golden-yellow and orange blossoms. However, they weren't the first living things to
catch my eye. No more than six inches away from the first pot
was a frenetic swarm of metallic blue-green bees. Every few
seconds one or two insects would leave the buzzing cloud and
alight on a fully opened flower of *L. cruenta.* The bee would
wander over the petals or crawl down the flower's "throat."
The bee scratched at the smooth floral surface and apparently
tucked something into the large "saddle bags" on each hind
leg before it rejoined the glittering throng.

The bees, I've since learned, were all males and they were
collecting "essence of orchid." I had blundered into one of
life's rare moments witnessed by only a handful of blissfully
lucky scientists over the past three decades. In fact, there are
those who would insist that memory has failed me and I could
never have seen a hovering mass of males at all. The situation
is *that* controversial.

The euglossini, or orchid bees, are a remarkable tribe
found from southern Texas to Argentina. *Euglossa* means
long tongue, and it's typical for both males and females to
have mouthparts longer than their bodies. Bees can't roll up
their tongues like butterflies, so they have to be tucked between the insects' legs when not in use. The tongue protrudes
beyond the tip of the bee's abdomen. Consequently, when a
euglossine hovers before a flower, it looks like a witch on her
broom.

Male euglossines are not the lazy, coddled drones associated with commercial honeybees. They feed themselves as
adults and with their long mouthparts can take nectar from
tubular and funnel-shaped flowers. As with most bees,
though, male euglossines do not collect pollen to feed to
offspring (that's "woman's work"), so their hind legs lack
pollen baskets. Instead, the tibia has been modified to form
a swollen vessel with a hairy slot that functions as a sort of
perfume flask. If the males collect and store odor particles

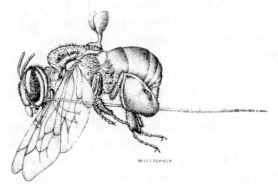

A male euglossine bee may have mouthparts longer than his body, and the "knees" of each hind leg are perfume flasks. Fragrant oils gathered from orchid petals are deposited in a slot on each flask. The pollen wads (pollinia) of the *Lycaste* are deposited on his back as he backs out of the flower.
ILLUSTRATION BY W. W. DELANEY

from such odd sources as mushrooms, tree saps, and the flowering stalks of tropical plants related to philodendrons (aroids), why do you think we call them orchid bees? Euglossines have been recorded harvesting the floral fragrances of almost a hundred fifty orchid species. Throughout the tropical Americas there are probably thousands of orchid species pollinated by euglossines in exchange for perfume.

Lycaste orchids have the rich scent of those tropical flowers preferred by male euglossines. They smell strongly of oil of cloves or something like cinammon mixed with medicated petroleum jelly. In fact, if you want to attract euglossines, you can rub a salve like Vicks VapoRub on a board and wait for the bees to congregate! When the bee alights on a *Lycaste* flower, it finds the scent glands and scratches out the volatile chemicals, which it transfers to the flasks on its hind legs. When the bee enters the floral throat he finds himself in a narrow cul-de-sac, and he must exit by backing out. As he does so he knocks off the anther cap hiding the pollen balls (pollinia), which become glued to his back. The next time the same bee exits from a different blossom on a different plant, the pollen balls will be deposited in the scoop-shaped tip of the pistil, and cross-pollination will be completed.

What does an orchid bee want with orchid perfumes? An earlier generation of scientists thought it was a sort of narcotic, as the males received no edible reward, like sweet nectar, and such bees seemed to lose all sense of caution while they were scraping up the oily essences. This "bee cocaine" explanation has been rejected. We've also scrapped such theories as the flowers smell like the bodies and nest holes of female bees, or fragrance chemicals prolong the bee's life.

Over a quarter of a century of observations and field experiments by such orchid luminaries as Cal Dodson, Robert Dressler, and Norris Williams have not yet given us a complete answer. We do know that the bees require pungent chemicals to complete some aspect of their social life. Each species creates its own unique cologne. It's possible the cologne of the male bee attracts the appropriate female. Other scientists have suggested that the cologne attracts other males. Once enough males assemble, they rise into the air and perform a loud and colorful "humming dance" to attract the attention of the females. That's what I thought I saw, but I can't recall seeing any bees stop and mate.

Each euglossine species may have to visit several different orchids to complete the appropriate formula. Different orchid species flowering at the same time often share the same male bee. For example, *L. aromatica* shares *Euglossa viridissima* with some *Gongora* and *Mormodes* orchids. When they flower together in the same forest the different orchids do not cross with each other, because the design of each flower ensures that it attaches its pollen balls to different parts of the bee's body. Catch a euglossine at a baited "odor trap" and you may find it wearing pollen wads of one orchid species on its eye, another on its leg, and a third on its thorax or abdomen. Exchanging clunky ornaments containing plant sperm is the price a male bee pays for his sexy after-shave.

Considering the wholesale destruction of the tropical American forests, a number of *Lycaste* species remain in danger of extinction. Cool, fertile mountain slopes are ideal for coffee plantations or popular cold-zone crops like peaches and strawberries. The rapacity of some orchid collectors isn't helping things. National forest preserves and parks in Costa Rica and Brazil must post special guards to protect orchids from thieves posing as tourists, or is it tourists posing as thieves? Flesh is weak, though, and I've read some accounts of collectors boasting that guards will direct them to choice lycastes for a small gratuity. As a member of the International Union for the Conservation of Nature, I have suggested a worldwide ban on the importation of *all* wild *Lycaste* species, because you really can't distinguish between rare and common plants when they're not in flower.

Therefore, when purchasing a *Lycaste* check that the plant has been grown from seed or by any tissue-culture technique. There are enough *Lycaste* species and their hybrids in long-term cultivation in Western countries to please all but the most fanatical grower. Furthermore, a *Lycaste* grown in a reputable nursery is far less likely to harbor unseen pests and diseases.

I helped to enter the rare *L. suaveolens* on the IUCN's Red Data list. This lovely yellow-and-orange-flowered species is confined to a few volcanic peaks in El Salvador. It's probably the only orchid to have enjoyed supernatural protection.

The Cerro Cacaquatique was converted into a series of coffee plantations decades ago. Only the peak of the dead volcano retained its native flora. The center of the peak offers a shallow, old, green sulfur lake. The forest colonized the inner escarpment of the cone and *L. suaveolens* plants could be found on boulders and tree limbs. Few peasants entered this forest to collect wood. The smell of the lake was foul, but people from the village down the mountain seemed to be in greater fear of some sort of "presence." It was believed that the spirit of a vindictive Indian princess dwelled in the water, and the lake had been the site of a tribal village. When the chief had not allowed his daughter to marry the man of her choice, she cursed her people, and the sulfur waters arose to destroy them all. She is still believed to claim two victims a year, and rumors persist about woodcutters who have vanished . . .

While I was a visiting professor of botany at the University of El Salvador, back in the mid-seventies, the herbarium director, Edy Montalvo, and I spent a day at Cacaquatique counting orchids and exploring the forest. The area was almost silent, but I doubt that many birds or larger animals could tolerate the sulfur fumes indefinitely. On the way back I turned to Edy and said in a playful tone, "There, now, I told you we had nothing to worry about." "Of course not," she replied in an uncharacteristically low voice. "Didn't you hear them say in the village that She has already taken her two for the year?"

Have an orchid, dearie?

CHAPTER 11

Steel Magnolias?

The famous Fountain of Youth, if I am rightly informed, is situated in the southern part of the Floridian Peninsula, not far from Lake Macaco. Its source is overshadowed by several gigantic magnolias, which, though numberless centuries old, have been kept fresh as violets by virtue of this wonderful water.

Nathaniel Hawthorne, "Dr. Heidegger's Experiment"

The March sunlight made the white flower buds look beautiful even in death. As the stiffened blossoms sparkled in their glassy shrouds of ice, their tops encrusted with snow, I could not help thinking of Snow White in her glass coffin.

There could be no happy ending here. As the temperature rose, the defrosted buds collapsed and browned. Within a few days the tree looked as if it were covered with rotting starfish. This spectacle seems to occur every two or three years within the grounds of the Missouri Botanical Garden, and throughout the city. Ah, how unlike the suburban gardens around Sydney, where the buds of soulangeana magnolias swell by midwinter (July) and remain in glorious flower into August.

Warm thaws through late February followed by March blizzards are hardly unique to St. Louis, and it's the price many

Americans pay for attempting to grow exotic plants along unpredictable margins of survival. Most breeds of Asian magnolias descend from species distributed through the milder, temperate forests of Japan and the mountainous, often subtropical, borders of China. Winters there may be intense but brief, and the rapid development of magnolia buds seems to be cued, in large part, by a short cold cycle followed by a series of "dependably" warmer days. The most common Asian species always produce their flowers on bare twigs before their leaves appear. That's why cold, early springs in North America often blast the flowers of Asian breeds, but their leaves survive, since they shouldn't reach full maturity until flowering ceases. A respite of just a couple of weeks allows the tender foliage to avoid the majority of late freezes.

That's a useful way to discriminate between the eight *Magnolia* species native to the southeastern regions of the United States and most of the common Asian stock. The American species do not crowd many flowers onto bare branches. Flowering usually occurs weeks *after* their leaves have expanded. In fact, the common bull bay *(M. grandiflora)* is an evergreen, so you never see either the flowers or autumn fruits free of the wide, glossy leaves. American species tend to stagger their flower buds, often over a period of months, so there is a self-replacing smattering of blossoms within the branches, instead of one explosive bouquet each spring.

Hawthorne's image of giant, immortal magnolias concealing the Fountain of Youth may have a scientific parallel. The fossil evidence is so good we suspect that magnolias flowered long before there was a human race to pick them. Ironically, it is only through the efforts of mankind that magnolias have been restored to much of their ancient territory.

When Drs. David Dilcher and Peter Crane reconstructed and described fossils of flowering branches from sandy beds on Linnenberger's ranch in Kansas back in 1984, they extended the heritage of magnolialike plants back to the mid-

Cretaceous Period (ninety-five to ninety-eight million years ago). Now, I would never suggest that *Archeanthus* (Greek *archae* means first; *anthos* means flower) *linnenbergeri* represents the remains of a "primeval" magnolia. I cannot even say that *Archeanthus* was the ancestor of our modern magnolias. This Cretaceous Period plant may be an extinct "cousin" of the family and not a "grandmother."

What would happen, though, if you could place the reconstructed fossil beside a living magnolia and other members in the magnolia family, like the tulip tree *(Liriodendron tulipifera)*? I think you would be forced to unite both living and extinct specimens on their broad similarities rather than separating them on their minor differences. That's precisely what Dilcher and Crane did. Most of the major differences between *Archeanthus* and living magnolias relate to the structure of their little seed boxes (pistils). The ripe ovaries of *Archeanthus* did not split open in the same way as that of a modern magnolia. Each *Archeanthus* pistil was connected to the central lump of floral tissue by means of its own little stalk. Those stalks are absent in the pistils of living magnolias, as their plump ovaries press directly onto the lump of floral tissue.

Fossil wood and seeds of the magnolia family have been recovered that can be dated from the end of the Cretaceous Period (about seventy million years ago). Fossil pollen of modern magnolias dates back around forty to fifty million years, and additional pollen grains, leaf fragments, and bark bits have been retrieved from amber. The most extraordinary magnolia fossils are only seventeen to twenty million years old. The leaves of extinct *Magnolia latahensis* may be rather recent in terms of magnolia history, but they are genetic treasures from another era, since they were still green when the rocks were split open! DNA fragments were extracted from these preserved leaves that contain a gene still found in living magnolias. Millions of years ago these leaves sank to the

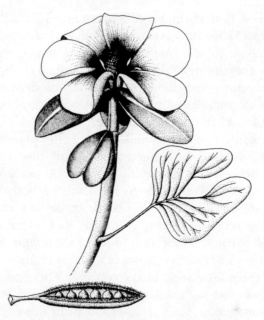

This reconstructed branch of *Archeanthus linnenbergeri* may resemble a modern magnolia, but take a closer look.
Above. There were three leafy organs (bracts) beneath each flower and each foliage leaf resembled a cloven hoof.
Below. Each fruit had its own distinct stalk (none of these features is found in living magnolias). ILLUSTRATION BY W. W. DELANEY.

bottom of a cold, oxygen-poor lake in what today is northern Idaho. The leaves were covered by thick layers of sediments. This initial combination of low temperatures and oxygen-poor ooze slowed the deterioration of the leaves before the lake dried up.

If you see a magnolia in a park or garden in any part of Europe, California, Canada, Russia, or even Idaho, it must have been planted by the hand of man. Even so, the fossil evidence is quite specific. Until a geologically short time ago the Northern Hemisphere wore an unbroken garland of magnolias. What could have happened?

Since magnolias are found in warm temperate to tropical zones, they could never survive the crushing cycles of glaciers and long, bitter winters that afflicted the Northern Hemisphere through the Pleistocene Epoch. The last great wave of glaciation began to retreat only eighteen thousand years ago, and the actual withdrawal process took an additional six thousand years. Magnolias survived in natural refuges that avoided the worst excesses of the Ice Age. These include the southeastern parts of both the United States and Asia. That's why some of the trees and wildflowers from South Carolina to Louisiana have much more in common with the vegetation of southern China or Japan than they do with the lands west of the Mississippi River or the countries of Europe.

As the northern half of this planet warmed up and the forests began to expand out from their Ice Age refuges, magnolias were still restricted from reclaiming many of their old haunts. Look at the climate of the United States, for example. Winters are still too cold north of the Mason-Dixon line. West of the Mississippi the land becomes hotter and drier favoring true prairies, deserts, and chaparral. Experiments have shown that magnolia seedlings cannot compete with the fast-sprouting, fibrous root systems of grasses. That's a good reason why you should never allow your lawn grass to grow right up to the stems of magnolia saplings and shrublets.

I also suspect that magnolias failed to spread through more northern forests due to the unique way in which they disperse their seeds. When the fruiting "cone" of a magnolia ripens in autumn, each separate ovary opens along a single slit, and one or two seeds tumble out. They don't fall very far. Each seed dangles by fibers that connect the seed to the interior of the ovary wall hanging by the remains of its old "umbilical cord." While the funiculus stalk of acacias becomes succulent and edible (Chapter 9), the magnolia's stalk becomes dry. Animals still play an important role in seed dispersal, though.

The cells of the outer lobe of most seeds unite and harden

to form a dead but protective dry husk. The cells of the outer lobe of a magnolia seed live to become a fleshy coat. This coat, or sarcotesta, is often a vivid red orange and it is very oily. The coat's aroma is nice and spicy and tastes a bit like wintergreen, in my opinion.

Migrating songbirds play the role of obstetrician, freeing the magnolia seeds from their cords before swallowing them whole or pecking off the flesh. Oily seeds are relished along autumn flyways, since fatty insects have been killed by frosts. The seeds are not harmed going through the guts of a cedar waxwing or a robin, as a hard layer has formed under the meaty one. Of course, if birds drop magnolia seeds while they're flying south through America or Asia, the next generation of trees won't become established north of their parents. That, I think, is why some of the 125 *Magnolia* species are found only in places like Cuba, Mexico, or western Malaysia. They are the descendents of the few seeds to have escaped the old refuges in southeastern America and Asia.

Charles Tubesing, a horticulturalist with the Holden Arboretum in Ohio, insists that growing magnolias from seed is not difficult, provided you follow a few simple steps. First, you must do what the birdies do: Strip off the seed's layer of colored flesh. That's easiest if you let it soak in water for a couple of days. Plant organs with fatty tissues are susceptible to bacteria and fungi, so magnolia seeds go rancid quickly if they are not gobbled up by passing birds in the wild. Cleaned, air-dried seeds are then planted in plastic sandwich bags filled with some sort of sterile potting mixture. Seal the bags and pop them in the vegetable keeper of your refrigerator for two to three months.

The seeds in the fridge are physically dormant but chemically active and are going through a process known as after-ripening. They were not really ready to sprout when they popped out of their parents' ovaries. A couple of months at low temperatures gives enzymes a chance to "catch up." This is a rather common stage in the life-cycles of flowering trees and shrubs we regard as comparatively primitive. In nature, the litter of the forest floor keeps the magnolia seed insulated yet cool in winter. Once the seeds come out of the vegetable keeper, they can be transferred to regular flowerpots, covered with soil, and watered. If you cover each pot with plastic wrap, you won't have to water it again until the shoots appear after a month. An additional month may seem a bit long to wait, but slow germination is normal in primitive flowering plants.

It's no surprise that the Chinese were the first to bring magnolias out of the woodlands and into their gardens as early as the seventh century A.D. They often grew them in large, ornamental containers and learned that they could be forced into early bloom if the wintered pots were moved to warm, protected sites. The Chinese have also prized the reproductive organs of their magnolias as herbal remedies. Pickled flower buds in vinegar and young fruits were given to people with bad coughs and lung infections. The seeds were eaten to reduce fever and treat chronic rheumatism. It's more than likely that magnolias are still prized by the "barefoot doctors" of rural China.

Western civilization did not even begin to develop until long after magnolias were extinct throughout Europe. The American species were the first to reclaim that region, entirely through man's unwitting fascination with the flowers. The sweet bay *(M. virginiana)* arrived in England around 1688, when a Virginia parson, John Bannister, sent a mixed collection of living plants to Henry Compton, the bishop of London. John Bartram, a Philadelphia Quaker, botanized through much of colonial America in the eighteenth century, and is credited with introducing more than two hundred plant species to Britain, including the bull bay *(M. grandiflora)*.

For a brief time the Yankee magnolias enjoyed great favor, as these grand trees, with their large white flowers, complemented Georgian architecture. It didn't last. Toward the end of the eighteenth century and on through the nineteenth, great plant collectors like Carl P. Thunberg, Sir Joseph Banks, and John Gould Veitch sent home a seemingly endless array of Asian magnolias. The yulan *(M. denudata)* and the lily magnolia *(M. liliflora)* did not grow into unmanageable titans up to fifty feet high like the sweet bays and bull bays. Changing tastes favored compact shrubs and small trees that flowered in one massive pink or white display. Furthermore, Asian magnolias could be "improved" by hybridization. The first soulangeana flowered in 1826 at the château of the chevalier M. Soulange-Bodin, near Paris. This mother of so many new forms was based on a spontaneous cross between a yulan and a lily magnolia sharing the same bed. The botanic gardens of Europe continued to send lucrative expeditions to China for new magnolias and other plants, until war and politics killed such programs by the late 1930s. It's only in the last few years that the Chinese government has welcomed foreign collectors willing to explore their southern forests bordering Myanmar (formerly Burma) and Laos.

You've probably guessed by now that the name magnolia may have a romantic appeal (remember Captain Andy's daughter, Magnolia, in the musical *Showboat?*) but it's a purely French concoction. Yes, both the genus *Magnolia* and the family Magnoliaceae were named to honor the same Pierre Magnol mentioned back in Chapter 3. Magnol seems to have lived an unromantic life compared to any fictional namesake. Persecuted as a Protestant, he took refuge at the garden of the University of Montpellier. His conversion to Catholicism in 1694 removed the last obstacle to both his promotion to professor and his directorship of the botanical garden (we academics will do anything for tenure). Magnol was honored by botanist Charles Plumier, not for seeing the true light, but rather for his contribution to the basic princi-

Above. Sun orchids like this Queen of Sheba *(Thelymitra variegata)* bloom in mid-spring deceiving bees collecting pollen for offspring. PHOTO BY BERT WELLS

Above. There are probably more orchids with blue flowers in Australia than anywhere else in the world. Here a blue fairy *(Caladenia deformis)* emerges between the heath twigs. PHOTO BY J. KELLY

Below. Arrowsmith orchid *(Caladenia crebra)* is closely related to the blue fairy, but it is modified to deceive its pollinators with a sex trap. The male wasp attempts to mate with the "fake female" sculpted on the lip petal (this male wasp is carrying yellow pollen globs from another orchid). PHOTO BY BERT WELLS

ples of plant classification. Isn't it appropriate that such an ancient family carries his name?

What do we love most about magnolia flowers: their impressive shapes, their glossy colors, or their evocative scents? A few species, like *M. stellata*, have spreading, flattened flowers like saucers or giant snowflakes. Most of the remaining species form bowls or urns. Both effects are achieved by simple organs. Unlike the flowers of most plants, a magnolia blossom cannot be broken into an outer cup of leaflike sepals and a larger, inner "crown" of petals. Instead, there are six to eighteen petallike structures known as tepals. Magnolia tepals never fuse with one another to form a united cup, tube, or trumpet, as in more advanced flowers. In the center of the magnolia flower is an elongated lump of tissue known as the receptacle. The numerous sexual organs are attached to this receptacle like steps in a spiral staircase. The skinny, flat stamens are around the base of the spiral and they "unzip themselves" when ripe to shed their pollen. The tiny pistils make up the glittering cone or pyramid on the apex of the receptacle. These pistils often secrete a nectarlike substance while they wait for pollen. This makes them glisten in a good light, and at least one American photographer has called them "the tower of jewels."

Magnolia color is something of a cheat, as there are no white pigments in flowers. "White" light passes through the transparent skin of the tepals and reflects off the starch granules in the lower layers of storage cells. The yellowish blush of some bull bays and virtually all the magnificent pink-through-purple effects we see tinting the outside of the tepals can be attributed to no more than three or four distinct compounds. Note that most magnolias lack distinct spots or stripes of color on the inside of the flowers. Such markings, or nectar guides, are used by insects to find their way within a flower. Some pollination biologists have remarked how bees

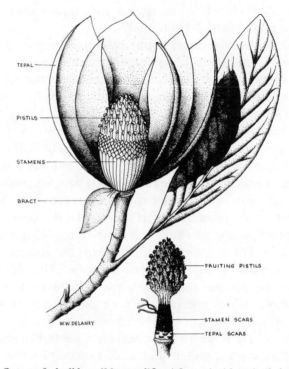

TEPAL

PISTILS

STAMENS

BRACT

FRUITING PISTILS

STAMEN SCARS

TEPAL SCARS

W.W.DELANEY

Above. A flower of a bull bay *(M. grandiflora)* forms inside a single bract that pops off as the tepals expand. Beetles hide and mate inside a secret chamber, eating pollen shed by many stamens and drinking from the pistil tips all attached to the same central post.

Below. Once the tepals and stamens drop off, the scarred central post (receptacle) is bare except for its cone of ripening pistils. ILLUSTRATION BY W. W. DELANEY

in magnolia blossoms seem "ill at ease . . . like a small child in a big bed." Fieldwork has shown that honeybees and moths often fail to find their way out of the half-opened globes of American magnolias, and they die of exposure.

The Chinese enjoy magnolias so much that they've dried the tepals of yulan to scent their tea. In fact, recent research suggests that it's the base of the floral receptacle (where the stamens are attached) that most often serves as the region of intense odor production. Magnolias may be bland watercolorists but they are arch perfumers. In 1975, botanist Leonard Thien and chemists W. H. Heimermann and Ralph Holman published their analysis of the fragrance of the eight American species, identifying forty-four substances. Different species offered different aromas and that meant different blends of the basic components. For example, the rather stinking flowers of the cucumber tree *(M. acuminata)* depended heavily on hydrocarbons. The pleasantly sweet blooms of the umbrella tree *(M. fraseri)* were based on a mixture of spicy terpenes and fruity methyl esters.

No wonder my father told me that children called magnolias "lemon smellers" when he was growing up in Brooklyn. The smell of the huge blossoms of the bull bay is reminiscent of fresh citrus peel. More than a century ago physicians were still warning their patients that they risked headaches, nausea, and nervous attacks if they slept in a closed room containing a vase of magnolia flowers, as their scent was overpowering. That seems a bit severe; in fact, I am grateful to whoever planted the grove of sweet bay outside the fence to Henry Shaw's tomb at the Missouri Botanical Garden. Linda and I always passed these young trees on our evening walks, and the St. Louis air smelled so refreshing even if only a single flower was evident.

Most magnolias appear to have turned their flowers into restaurants-*cum*-motels to accommodate a rather coarse clientele. They appear to be pollinated by beetles, including a few weevils (Curculionidae) and members of such peculiar families as the false blister beetles (Oedemeridae), leaf beetles (Chrysomelidae), jewel beetles (Buprestidae), tumbling flower beetles (Mordellidae), rove beetles (Staphylinidae), and sap beetles (Nitidulidae). It's possible that the sap beetles have an ancient relationship with the magnolia family, as casts of the shells of such beetles have been found to predate *Archeanthus.*

Beetles are attracted by the piercing odors and are quite at home inside the dim chambers of the magnolia's flowers, even when they shut up at night. Inside the closed flower there is plenty of pollen to eat or secretions to drink. More than a thousand beetles can be found inside a single flower of bull bay, so there are plenty of opportunities for these insects to select their own mates and copulate under the relative security of the "tepal tent." A beetle may leave a magnolia flower carrying pollen between the hairs on its undersurface. Cross-pollination can occur when a thirsty, pollen-laden insect enters the flower of a second tree and drinks from one of the receptive pistils. A magnolia flower secretes pistil nectar and then dries up its pistil tips before it ever releases its own pollen. This prevents self-pollination within the same flower if beetles are pollen hungry *and* nectar thirsty. If you think it's a rather sloppy process, you may be pleased to learn that an earlier generation of naturalists called it "mess and spoil pollination."

Magnolias have such a long history it's hard to reconcile the fact that their immediate future is very tied up with such an irritating upstart as *Homo sapiens.* You'd think that our love affair with these trees and shrubs has lasted so long that they will always be treasured. I'm not so sure. One of the ugliest memories of my childhood on the South Shore of Long Island was the frequent sight of new neighbors chopping down twenty- or thirty-year-old magnolias planted by previous owners. No one liked the chore of raking up the dead tepals in May. The trees were regarded as unclean by anal-retentive suburbanites, as discolored tepals, wind-strewn on a lawn, reminded the owners of old banana skins.

How does the song go?—"Everything old is new again." At the moment, magnolias are "in" plants with the gardening set in the Australian state of Victoria. Grand tours of British gardens have given Aussies a taste for the white-and-gray garden schemes of Vita Sackville-West. A white magnolia is *de rigueur.* So we go from fad to fad, and that's not a terrible thing. Somewhere in the world there will always be a place for moonlight and magnolias.

PART FIVE

The People's Plants

CHAPTER 12

Columbines, Cuckolds, and National Controversy

Bring hither the Pink and purple Columbine
 With Gillyflowers:
Bring Coronation, and Sops in wine,
 Worn of paramours.

Edmund Spenser, *The Shephardes Calendar* (April)

Pity the Victorian gentleman who is handed a single red columbine by a silent young woman. How should he interpret the language of flowers? Was this her shy way of hinting, "I grow anxious and tremble in your presence," or did she give him a cruel message that said, "What folly, your wife is sleeping with someone else!"?

The idea that every little flower has a meaning all its own has been shared by many cultures over many epochs. Some long traditions of floral symbolism have resulted in great art. Our museums treasure the still lifes of the Dutch Masters. The Japanese practice ikebana, the most subtle yet structuralized form of flower arrangement. Both art forms have one thing in common: they can be admired for their compositions and use of colors, or they can be appreciated as allegories reflecting spirituality and moral strength.

The wild columbines of Europe have been painted since

the Middle Ages. The flowers nod and tremble in the breeze, and that was considered a sign of humility. More important, though, generations of Europeans had looked at columbines and seen five little doves feeding from the same dish. Columbine, after all, is from the Latin *columba*, for dove, and the association is quite old. Chaucer would have known this flower as the culverwort, cullenby, or cullavine—all Old English words meaning wild pigeon plant. Combine the unique shape of the columbine with its heavenly blue to royal purple colors and you had a potent symbol of the Holy Ghost.

You can see the five birds in a blossom for yourself if you look at a garden flower bred from the most common European species, *Aquilegia vulgaris*. See where the flower connects to its stalk? There are five winglike sepals. In between each pair of sepals a petal has pushed up a hollow spur. The spur has a curving neck that bends toward the floral stalk. Each spur ends in a beaky knob, completing the illusion of a circle of five pigeons, wing to wing, all pecking at the same source.

Now you can see why columbines popped up on religious panels and frescoes, although they were never given the prominence, say, of the madonna lily in depictions of the Annunciation. To emphasize the Trinity some artists would paint three columbine flowers on three separate stalks that grew out of the same stem base. How, then, did a symbol of a Christian mystery become so debased that it represented the breaking of marital vows?

The language of flowers became really popular with British and French women early in the last century. When you received a bouquet from a friend or intimate, you were expected to decipher a message or whole sentence from the arrangement of species. Art historian Sam Segal has written that many flower symbols changed during the Romantic period. Some species were given new meanings so they could emphasize individual relationships. It seems that English pas-

Fair Columbines that drew the car of Venus from her distant star:

Author/illustrator Walter Crane (1845–1915) turned flowers into puns. *Columbine* is Latin for dove, and doves were sacred to Venus. Crane follows the folk tradition turning the five spurs of each flower into pigeon heads and the sepals into wings. BAILLEAU LIBRARY, UNIVERSITY OF MELBOURNE

tors, in particular, established a successful cottage industry by writing books about flower words for the sentimentally inclined. These men combed old poetry, mythology, and regional folklore so that different flowers could be converted into a "science of sweet things" for an avid readership.

Columbines offered a number of possibilities, since not everyone who looked at the spurs saw pigeon heads and necks. Some saw columbines as articles of clothing, such as the belled hat of a court jester, the Virgin's glove (*gant de Notre-Dame*), two faces under a hat, Jack in trousers or in baggy, quivering pairs of pants *(Schlotterhose)*. Cultivated columbines are still marketed as granny bonnets. People have seen the columbine's spurs as the claws of an eagle. That gives us the scientific name for the genus, *Aquilegia* (Latin *aquila* means eagle). There's also a mythological touch in a German name for columbine *(Jovisblume)*, since the eagle was sacred to Jove, king of the gods.

That takes us to the Reverend Hilderic Friend, who wrote *Flowers and Flower Lore*, published back in 1884. Rev. Friend said that columbines were the flowers of deserted lovers and had been symbols of cuckoldry before 1600. Of course, the columbine's spurs were the cuckold's horns. Other authors noticed that astrologers had placed the columbine under the dominion of the planet Venus, and everyone knew she was no better than she should've been.

Columbines (*Aquilegia* species) belong to the family of buttercups and anemones (Ranunculaceae). Flowers in this family may conceal their nectar in pouches or tubes made of sepals or petals, and their odd shapes are sometimes reflected in common names. The columbine is related to another blossom that has only a single sepal spur that has been compared to a dolphin *(Delphinium)* or bird's toe (larkspur). In contrast, one sepal of an *Aconitum* forms such a large hood the plants are often known as monkshoods.

That's where the mystery of the unfaithful columbine

should end, but I'm not so sure. Gardeners have noticed for centuries that the offspring of one columbine often grow into plants that look quite different from their seed mother. Such observations come down from a time long before people understood that flowers are sexual organs. Remember the character of Columbine in French and Italian comedy? She is not the abandoned one. She is the deceiver who pretends love for Pierrot but whose affections are really spent on the invisible Harlequin.

Vita Sackville-West, the great gardener and author, got it right over half a century ago. She found columbines irresistible but couldn't resist quoting one of her nurserymen's sniffier remarks about such flowers: "Their morals leave much to be desired."

The loose morals of these plants became really apparent after 1650 when the first of the New World columbines reached Europe. These were the rock bells or cluckies *(A. canadensis)* still common through the eastern half of Canada and the United States. There are about seventy species of wild columbines found in the cooler recesses of the Northern Hemisphere, but the most striking flowers must come from North America. This is not a matter of national pride. All but one of the European species have flowers that are blue, pink-purple, or white. Such flowers have a wide, flouncy skirt and the spurs are relatively short. Only American species, like *A. canadensis,* come in bright reds. If you want to see a native columbine with yellow flowers in Europe you have to go all the way to Bulgaria to find *A. aurea.* American columbines often tint their floral openings with gold and, as you move to the Southwest, you can find columbines that are a pure pale yellow, like *A. chrysantha.* American columbines tend to have shapely, narrow flowers ending in the longest, most elegant, swans' necks.

The rock bell with its almost straight scarlet spurs and slender yellow borders made quite a splash at the court of

Above. The yellow columbine *(A. chrysantha)* has the longest spreading spurs and a pale gold horizontal flower receiving hovering hawkmoths. *Lower left.* The rockbell *(A. canadensis)* has shorter, erect, bundled spurs and a red nodding flower receiving hummingbirds that hover underneath. *Lower right.* The European columbine *(A. vulgaris)* has the shortest spurs, with hooked tips and a purple nodding flower receiving bees that cling upside down to floral organs. These three species may hybridize when grown in the same garden bed and visited by the same local pollinators.
ILLUSTRATIONS BY J. MYERS

Charles I. Clumps of rock bells were far more difficult to sustain year after year than the weedier *A. vulgaris* that had begun its career as a wayside flower wandering in and out of gardens like cats. But, wait a minute . . . what was this? Grow rock bells *(A. canadensis)* and common columbines *(A. vulgaris)* on the same turf and the rock bells seemed to "degenerate" after only one generation. Their seeds produced much hardier plants, but the rock bell's offspring had shorter, crooked spurs and bold reds faded out or muddied to magenta.

Today we understand that the honeybees and bumblebees visiting garden beds in which different columbine species grow make few distinctions between color or national origin. They take pollen indiscriminately from American and European species. Seeds developing in a withering rock bell may have a common columbine for a father, or vice versa. Pollination biologist Lazarus Walter Macior repeated the bee-driven dalliances of the columbines in an Ohio garden more than twenty-five years ago. He grew at least five kinds of columbines together (both true species and hybrids) and then photographed the acts of infidelity as they all came into bloom.

Bumblebees collected pollen from the different columbines, dusting the pistil tips of different flowers with foreign genes. Lapping nectar was another matter, though. The tongues of some bumblebee species couldn't reach the sweet reward hidden in the tips of the longest, straightest spurs and both workers and queens "lost their patience" with the artful flowers. Instead of dangling upside down and shoving their tongues correctly up each petal entrance, the bees bit holes in the spur tips. Now they could drink the nectar oozing from the wounds at their leisure, like six-legged Draculas.

As Europeans added new species of American columbines to their gardens the genetic mess increased. You can see this for yourself by sowing any packet of columbine seeds recommended for meadow gardens. The advertisers promise you true wildflowers, but don't believe it. The most variable flowers appear in which different shapes and colors meld into one another. Short spurs with purplish petals suggest a European ancestry, but the same blossom may have bright-red sepals—so a "grandparent" was probably a crimson columbine *(A. formosa)*. Do any flowers have light-blue spurs and white petal tips? If so, there must have been some past crossing to a Colorado blue or Rocky Mountain columbine *(A. caerulea)*. What about that plant with the longest golden spurs? Yellow columbines *(A. chrysantha)* have been used in hybridization since the middle of the last century.

Hybrid columbines show high degrees of fertility, unlike the hybrids of so many other flowering plants. Hybrid columbines set good seed if they cross with each other or mate with either of their parent species. What happens in the garden happens in the wild. Different columbine species tend to occupy different elevations along mountain ranges. Botanists have documented hybrid pockets along slopes in California and Colorado. Why haven't all seventy *Aquilegia* species combined into one?

The isolation of two columbine species is often just a matter of sheer distance. A columbine growing in the Swiss Alps has little opportunity of crossing with a plant in the Sierra Nevada. Bees are not expected to deliver pollen on intercontinental flights. Of course, that can't explain the partial isolation of three or four species of columbines on the same mountain.

The way in which different species maintain "separateness" has been a major interest of Verne Grant, one of the great American contributors to evolutionary biology. Over forty years ago Professor Grant explored interactions between Coville's columbine *(A. pubescens)* and the crimson columbine *(A. formosa)* of the West. Coville's columbine has creamy-white flowers that are held erect and trail spurs up to almost

Above. The shallow, bowllike flower of *Passiflora caerulea* advertises the blue-purple tints and exhibits the fine, spreading corona segments associated with bee pollination. PHOTO BY JIM LA VIGNE

Below. The tubular flower of *P. vitifolia* pulls back its long red petals, exposing a "picket fence" made by the corona. Note how the head of this hermit hummingbird *(Glaucis aenea)* is dusted with pollen by an overhanging anther when it rams its bill down the floral throat. PHOTO BY MICHAEL FOGDEN

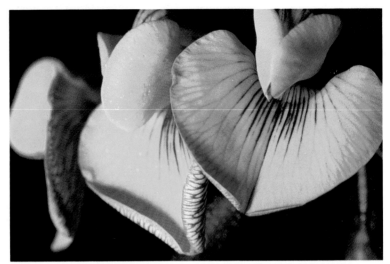

Above. Nectar guides in pea blossoms are "less direct" as both nectar and pollen are hidden inside folded, "keel" petal (under the two, clasping wing petals). Red-brown streaks on the wide, "banner" petal point the bee to the base of the keel petal where it can insert its tongue. PHOTO BY JAMIE PLAZA

Below. Black wattle *(A. mearnsii)* comes from Australia, but it shows the characteristics associated with acacias on other continents. The little flowers are arranged in balls, while the compound (bipinnate) leaves resemble plumes. PHOTO BY JAIME PLAZA

two inches in length. The crimson columbine has red, nodding flowers and its spurs are little more than a third the length of those of a Coville's columbine. When the two species hybridize, the offspring is a pinkish yellow, the flowers are held horizontally, and the spur length is midway between that of the two parent species. Research by later scientists has revealed that the hybrid even "mixes up" the amino acids found in the different nectars of its parents.

Two factors in the environment slow up the recombination of the crimson and Coville's columbines. First, as each species offers quite different fashions of flower presentation, each tends to appeal more to different pollinators. The crimson columbine tends to be a favorite of hummingbirds like the calliope *(Stellula calliope)* and the rufous hummingbird *(Selasphorus rufus)*. They forage for nectar by day and don't mind "helicoptering" under a nodding flower while their probing beaks enter the petal openings and their tongues seek out nectar in the spur knobs.

As the sun begins to set, out come the hawkmoths or sphinx moths like *Hyles lineata.* The pale flowers of Coville's columbine stand out in the gloom and the insect uncoils its long tongue to reach nectar hidden in the spur tips. It's not a perfect arrangement. The mountains are full of long-tongue bumblebees and they may retain their roles as columbine hybridizers.

Hawkmoths often visit crimson columbines, although it's unlikely they will be dusted with much pollen. The moth tongues are so much longer than the crimson spurs that their heads needn't contact the bunch of stamens while they shed their pollen. Hummingbirds visit Coville's columbine but they can't reach the nectar hidden in the long spurs, so they play Jack the Ripper and actually slash them open with their bills while avoiding the bunch of stamens.

The second reason why columbine hybrids do not appear to spread much and "swamp" the gene pools of their parents has something to do with soil and altitude limits. Coville's columbine likes windswept, rocky slopes, often above the timberline, where the soil is thin and sandy. The crimson columbine prefers lower altitudes, where it grows shaded by trees in thick, moist earth. Yes, you guessed it. Their hybrids need conditions intermediate between both parents, and this often relegates them to rather narrow stretches of land. If a hybrid seed isn't washed or blown away from its parent's habitat, it may not live long enough to flower. Ironically, that's why hybrid columbines do so well in cultivation. Few gardeners have either the space or energy to reproduce the sort of soil textures and chemistry associated with the movement of glaciers. As garden loams tend to be mixtures of "this and that," they encourage hybrids at the expense of true species.

The last time I wandered around my parents' neighborhood in Merrick, New York, I received the most pleasant surprise. Front gardens sported informal clumps of hybrid columbines peeking through the shrubbery. That's quite an improvement since my childhood, when families fled New York City for the suburbs. Long, bare strips of ground around the house were kept almost exclusively for annual plants like petunias, marigolds, and zinnias. These annuals were lined up in military rows or crammed into peeling wheelbarrows, "rustic" milk cans, and cracked, whitewashed tires (off Dad's Chrysler) to "add color" to the front lawn.

It's too bad more Americans didn't appreciate their columbines sooner. At the turn of this century there was a movement to make the columbine the national flower. Wouldn't columbines have been a distinct improvement over roses? They take up less space and they're much less expensive. As we've seen, the most beautiful columbines in the world are American species. The word *columbine* suggests Christopher Columbus. The common name embraces the dove of peace, while the scientific name includes the eagle, the bird of freedom. Unlike roses, columbines are native to almost every

American state (the mountain blue is the state flower of Colorado). Unlike roses, columbines come in red, white, *and* blue. Columbine nectar nourishes gemlike birds and some of our most beautiful moths. Roses don't even make nectar.

Did anyone but florists and nurserypersons benefit after the rose became America's national flower? *Profit* is not a dirty word and anyone who can make a living from commercial horticulture these days deserves our praise. The trouble is, well . . . you know, their morals leave much to be desired.

CHAPTER 13

The Life and Times of Daffy-Down-Dilly

For me, the high point came at Capri. My mother and Mrs Burton-Brown drove up to the little white town, but I walked. At once, I found myself surrounded by scented wild narcissi in flower, and I was shaken by a kind of ecstasy: it was one of the most moving and transporting experiences I ever enjoyed, more moving even than the Greek temples on their lonely hillsides.

Julian Huxley, *Memories*

After five years in St. Louis I began to hate the yellow-and-white bastards. They are such a visual cliché. Bulbs have been planted along the highways by massing them into huge, butterfly patterns. Over the years the soil shifts, butterfly wings grow rather moth-eaten, and the pattern degrades into a giant yellow bowtie.

You can't escape them in the city, either, as they've become symbols of urban renewal and the laudable cleanup campaign known as Operation Brightside. At St. Louis University the bulbs have been shoved under our few ornamental pear and crabapple trees. By the end of April my dean saunters over to the faculty lunch table and makes his annual pronouncement. "This is the most beautiful time of year on campus," he proclaims with the smug pride of a country squire surveying his lands and chattels. Of course, as St. Louis U. has never given its few flower beds much priority, that's not saying much.

It's also obvious that he isn't a frequent visitor to our medical school campus. Once the daffodils begin to blow, children from the adjacent slums invade and chop them to pieces. The cheerful sex organs are left to dry up on the concrete.

It's historically correct to call a daffodil a bastard. That's what the English once called their only native species *(Narcissus pseudonarcissus)*. It often takes a long time before people appreciate their own wildflowers. Britons once preferred imported bulbs of white asphodel *(Asphodelus albus)* and poet's narcissus, or affadil *(N. poeticus)*, because their stalks bear many pure white flowers. In contrast, the English plant produces only a solitary blossom and its yellowness made it unfashionable. Since the native flower lacked both the right form and color it was regarded, at best, as a "false" narcissus (hence the *pseudo* in *pseudonarcissus*) or a *bastard affadil*, as it lacked the legitimate features of *N. poeticus*. By the time Elizabeth I was on the throne *bastard affadil* had been softened to daffadille, daffadilly, and daffadowndylly.

English is an inventive tongue, though, and *N. pseudonarcissus* has also been called Lent Lily, yellow crow bells, churn flower, Sweet Nancy, bellrose, butter and eggs, giggary, and Ganymede's Cup. Sometimes I think it's a shame that only the word *daffodil* has really persisted.

Why are daffodils so omnipresent in almost every country with a temperate climate? They dominate public and private gardens from late winter through mid-spring. If you are depressed by months of ice and snow you are encouraged to force pots of daffodil bulbs on your windowsill. Make a donation to a charity or hospital and someone hands you a daffodil. As cut flowers in season they are bargains. Your local florist bundles them together like asparagus stalks and may dump them into plastic buckets to await purchase for a few dollars.

For one thing, daffodils have had a remarkably good press. Roses may be for romance, but daffodils seem to touch the imagination. Flower writers Alice Coats and Buckner Hollingsworth came to much the same conclusion—that poets tended to ignore these flowers until the Elizabethan era. That's not too surprising, as *daffodil* seems a far sweeter word than *false* or *bastard affadil.* Pick up any standard book of quotations. You'll find that poets insist that the daffodil is a better antidepressant than lithium, a more faithful companion than the family dog, and offers better performances and special effects than most movies.

Daffy-down-dilly dressed formally when she came to town for Mother Goose. The daffodil died early and on cue for English poet Robert Herrick; and the flowers burst into small, keen flames for American poet Lizette Reese. Tennyson wrote of a daffodil sky, while Masefield insisted that the month of April could be found inside a daffodil. *Daffodillies* mourn for Milton's friend by filling their cups with tears and strewing them on Lycid's hearse!

Life imitates art, and horticulturists persist in their attempts to reproduce Wordsworth's "choreographed" vision. At the Chicago Botanical Garden some original souls planted who knows how many bulbs "beside the lake, beneath the trees, fluttering and dancing in the breeze." It's seems as if no poet has ever had a nasty thing to say about these flowers—until I read an anthology of Australian verse and stumbled across "Daffodils" by Gina Ballyntyne. Written in this century, the opening lines alone damn with the faintest praise:

> Now you are nodding in every well-bred garden;
> Worn by the pretty girl in the omnibus;
> Sprouting seasonally in all the shop-windows

That yearly create synthetic spring for us.
You have been carefully coaxed to this blooming,
Cotton-wooled out of an unwilling soil—
You the delicate breath of northern April
Have become the bright reward of southern toil.

Ms. Ballyntyne goes on to condemn the yellow heads of daffodils for bringing "An alien spring." She yearned to return to the Australian bush and count the gold of *native* wildflowers. It takes a lot of guts to be critical of daffs, in my opinion. When has an American poet encouraged his or her audience to abandon daffs for spring forests filled with trilliums and toothworts? The trouble is that while Ms. Ballyntyne's sentiments are praiseworthy, her horticulture stinks.

Glamorizing a flower for five hundred years won't guarantee it a place in millions of gardens unless it's the hardiest of plants. The toughness of daffodils, and their narcissus and jonquil relatives, provides the second key to their popularity: They do *not* have to be coaxed and cotton-wooled out of unwilling soils. It has been my observation that these plants are often more enduring than the homesick Europeans who planted them. Visit some of the rural settlements through southeastern Australia where small farms have been deserted and eucalypt woodlands encroach. The lush daffodil clumps are in far better shape than the decayed huts or lonely, crumbling chimneys.

"Feral" daffodils comprise one of my strongest, earliest memories of Australia. Back in 1979, I was wandering lonely as a cloud along the back lanes of Healesville, Victoria. In the late August afternoon I stopped at a paddock to admire a mare racing with her foal. The horses looked magnificent against the deep-blue sky, and their pasture was filled with white- and green-flowered daffodils.

Did the horses' owner appreciate the scene? It could have ended in an expensive call to the veterinarian. Daffodils are rich in the alkaloid lycorine, and livestock sicken when they eat exposed bulbs. During World War II the Dutch tried unsuccessfully to use their bulbs as an animal fodder. People were also poisoned when they tried to substitute daff bulbs for onions. Not surprisingly, few native animals in Australia and North America attack daffodils even after these foreigners "escape" into the bush. Eelworms (nematodes), fungi, and fly maggots are the specialized enemies of daffodils. They have evolved with the plants in their original habitats and have hitchhiked around the world inside infected bulbs.

At least four species of European *Narcissus* have run wild through the United States (especially through the South) and people still treat them as familiar wildflowers, not as intruders. Tennessee Williams seems to have turned memories of *N. jonquila* into one of Amanda Wingfield's most plaintive anecdotes of her courtship days in *The Glass Menagerie*:

> So lovely, that country in May—all lacy with dogwood, literally flooded with jonquils! That was the spring I had the craze for jonquils. Jonquils became an absolute obsession. Mother said, "Honey, there's no more room for jonquils." And still I kept bringing in more jonquils. Whenever, wherever I saw them, I'd say, "Stop! Stop! I see jonquils!" I made the young men help me gather the jonquils! It was a joke, Amanda and her jonquils. Finally there were no more vases to hold them, every available space was filled with jonquils. No vases to hold them? All right, I'll hold them myself! And then I—met your father! Malaria fever and jonquils and then—this—boy . . .

Daffodils and their relatives do well throughout the American South and Australia because they prefer regions that experience mild, wet winters and hot summers. The majority of the twenty to twenty-four species of *Narcissus* are native to the Mediterranean basin, especially the far-western regions. Some of these wild species can't even tolerate extended freezes. Brian Mathew, scientific officer of the Royal Botanic Gardens at Kew, has warned would-be growers about importing such bulbs. They must be allowed to literally bake in harsh sandy or clay soils all summer long or they will not flower the following spring.

If you find it hard to think of daffs as the true wildflowers of Spain and Portugal, consider all those species found in northwestern Africa and some even scattered through the Atlas Mountains. Two botanists recently wrote that the future breeding of new garden daffodils and narcissi may depend ultimately on the untapped gene pools in Morocco! Meanwhile, I have not been unable to track down an earlier report that a dried wreath of narcissus was found in a three-thousand-year-old Egyptian tomb. However, in some Middle East countries the spring-flowering narcissus *(N. tazetta)* is often grown in Muslim cemeteries. In Algiers, some mourners may still bring bunches of narcissi to a loved one on Fridays, pick the starlike flowers from their stalks, then scatter them on the grave.

So we can see that although the wild daffodil, or Lent Lily *(N. pseudonarcissus)*, is native to England, it has never been confined exclusively to that chilly island. Venture across the English Channel and you will find it is more densely distributed through southern France into Spain, where it breaks up into eight dazzling subspecies.

Hyacinths and tulips tend to vanish after less than a decade in a garden bed unless their numbers are replanted. Although most daffodil bulbs have a life span of only four years, they may increase their numbers with time and they can do it without sex. Bulbs are not roots. Fibrous roots sprout from the base of the daff bulb during the growing season. Daffodil bulbs are underground stems in which the shoot is wrapped up in layers of fleshy storage "leaves" and then protected by scales and sheets of thin, dry leaves forming a sheath. Like most stems, a daffodil bulb can branch off new stems as lateral buds. These lateral buds form at the base of the old, mother "bulb" and eventually grow into new daughter bulbs that become independent when the mother bulb dies.

The daffodil literally clones itself. That's why gardeners are encouraged to "lift and separate" daughter bulbs every three or four years in some latitudes. When daffodil growers want to increase the numbers of a favored variety, they often scar or partially scoop out the base of a bulb and then replant it. Damage the base of the bulb and you wound or kill the stem shoot hidden inside. This stimulates the frenzied growth of daughter bulbs.

I have seen what happens, though, when daffodils and narcissi find soil to their liking, and gardeners fail to thin them out. When I lived in the rural town of St. Arnaud, Australia (northeast of Melbourne), for a couple of months, a friend invited me to see the cottage garden of an elderly couple. Several beds consisted almost exclusively of the dormant bulbs of daffs and narcissi. They were so dense that daughter bulbs had been pushed right out of the ground. My friend John told me that if I dug down into the bed I'd find that the bulbs went down almost a foot into the hot, dry earth. He was right.

Most daffodils require both a hot and cold signal before they flower. A month or less of temperatures in the eighties (warm storage) simulates the Mediterranean summers. Another six to eight weeks of low temperatures offers the "precooling" the bulb experiences in winter ground. Daffodils are such a big industry today that shifts in temperature are applied artificially so we can have them out of season.

This bulb trade offers two great advantages when promoting the popularity of daffodils with amateur gardeners. First, by summer, a mature, dormant bulb already contains the embryonic flower it will produce the next spring, provided it receives the appropriate environmental cues. Planting a bulb in autumn and seeing it flower six months later is a lot more satisfying than planting daffodil seeds and waiting years for the developing bulblet to reach flowering size. Daffodil bulbs are as easy to transport as onions, and they've been shipped all over the world with little fuss.

Second, when you cross different species of daffodils and narcissi, the result is often a beautiful but sterile offspring. These "mules" will still reproduce without sex by manufacturing daughter bulbs. In some parts of Europe daughter bulbs of sterile hybrids have pushed their way out of gardens and invaded mountain slopes and woodlands. Clones are often cherished for their sheer uniformity. Sometime in the seventh century A.D., a sterile hybrid based on the spring-flowering narcissus *(N. tazetta)*, which had probably been back-crossed with the hybrid orange narcissus *(N. x incomparibilis)*, was carried to China. Since it flowered in late winter, it became a charming addition to New Year festivities and has since been known as the New Year lily or good luck flower. The Chinese liked to force the bulbs in bowls of wet pebbles (as we do today), probably contributing to another quaint name, the water fairy flower.

This foreign, sterile blossom became a favorite of Chinese artists and poets. Go to the Chinese wing of the Metropolitan Museum of Art in Manhattan. You will find a thirteenth-century scroll depicting narcissi flowering by a brook. A poem was written on the scroll by Ch'iu Yuan (1247–1327?) in the days of the Mongol conquests. It laments that these flowers were the only things to live through the devastation of a barbarian invasion.

No one would care much about the ease of culturing daffodils if we found the flowers unattractive. That's obviously not the case, as the pleasure taken from the sight of daffodils and narcissi is enshrined as far back as the body of classical mythology. Homer thought the glittering flowers were a noble sight for both men and the immortal gods, so he included them in his "Hymn to Demeter." Everyone knows how

Narcissus was turned into a flower after he pined to death while yearning for his gorgeous reflection.

Less familiar, though, is the plant's role in the rape of Proserpina, the spring goddess. While reaching for an unknown purple-and-silver flower she was carried off to the underworld by her uncle Pluto. Scholars suspect this floral lure, created by Father Jupiter, was the pheasant's-eye or poet's narcissus *(N. poeticus)* with its white, petallike "tepals" and orange-red cup. The flowers crowned the head of both the mother goddesses and the avenging Furies.

Daffodils belong to a family of plants offering us some of our most spectacular flowers, the Amaryllidaceae. This includes "spring" bulbs that come up even earlier than daffodils, such as snowflakes *(Leucojum)* and snowdrops *(Galanthus)*. However, it also includes a number of warm-temperate and subtropical bulbs most readers will recognize only as pot plants: amaryllis *(Hippeastrum)*, clivias *(Clivia)*, spider lilies *(Pancratium)*, and crinum lilies *(Crinum)*, to name a few.

As you can see, daffodils and many members of the Amaryllidaceae are often confused with true lilies (Liliaceae). In fact, the flowers of daffs and other amaryllids employ a special structural trick. Their floral organs are mounted on top of the ovary and they usually fuse together forming a long tube known as the hypanthium. In true lilies the other floral organs do not become attached to the top of the ovary; they do not fuse into a hypanthium tube.

The length of the hypanthium tube is often increased by the development of a corona in daffodils. In a previous chapter, we've seen the fringed corona of the passionflower made up of loose, threadlike segments growing out of each petal. In daffodils, narcissi, and jonquils the corona is usually an erect, ruffled, but undivided "petticoat" made up of the fused outgrowths of each of the six tepals.

It's the corona that probably gives daffodils their undying

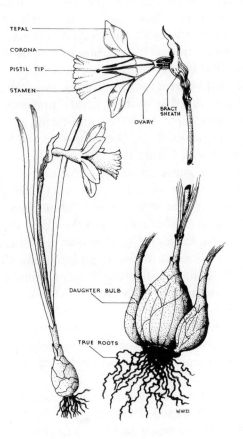

TEPAL

CORONA

PISTIL TIP

STAMEN

BRACT SHEATH

OVARY

DAUGHTER BULB

TRUE ROOTS

W.W.D.

Above. Sexual reproduction in daffodils requires that the base of the floral organs fuse into a tube (hypanthium) above the ovary. The tube forms a bonnet (corona) that controls the movements of drinking insects.
Below. Vegetative reproduction requires lateral buds at the base of the old bulb to develop into independent "daughters." ILLUSTRATION BY W. W. DELANEY

popularity. Few hardy bulbs offer any structure so unique. Corona length and shape may vary considerably among different members of the genus *Narcissus*. In *Narcissus humilis* the flower's corona is little more than a circle of low, ridged scales. Compare this with the cyclamen-flowered narcissus *(N. cyclamineus)*, in which the trumpetlike corona is actually longer than the hypanthium tube.

The daffodil's corona seems to have two functions. If you soak the flower in a dye, staining for the presence of aromatic oils, the corona turns brick red, indicating it's the flower's scent gland, or osmophore. The odors released by some coronas can be strong. I fully sympathize with the woman who visited a British gardener and complained that his vase of narcissi smelled like embalming fluid! Other people have remarked on the leathery or sooty "after tang." In the last century, Dr. J. E. Taylor compared the odor of jonquils and narcissus to naphthalene (the major ingredient in mothballs), and he thought he was complimenting the blossoms! The ancients believed that the flower's scent could numb people. No wonder that the words *narcissus* and *narcotic* have the same Greek origin.

Maybe there's an element of truth here. Obviously, the scent of narcissi "transported" the youthful Julian Huxley and kept his memory green when he was a dry, agnostic scientist.

The last word on the corona's smell belongs properly to Edward A. Bowles (1865–1954), a great breeder of *Narcissus*. He described the nutmeg and citrus-peel notes in daff perfumes and went so far as to compare the smell of one variety as "more like the scent in a chocolate box after the contents had vanished." Nevertheless, Bowles warned against poet's narcissus in a formal centerpiece, because the overpowering odor proves "disastrous to the palate . . . when too close to dinner plate and wineglass."

The corona also appears to act as a stiff barrier excluding

small, short-tongued insects that would steal the nectar secreted at the base of the stamen stalks without pollinating the flower. For so many daffodils and narcissi blooming in the mild, late winters or early spring, bumblebees *(Bombus)* may be the most important pollinators in their native habitats. Bumblebee tongues are long enough to reach the nectar at the base of the flower, and their fat, hairy bodies collide with the tips of the sexual organs as they ram their heads into the corona. The smaller, slender honeybees *(Apis)* can reach the nectar, but many daffodil breeders complain they fail to contact the pollen or the pistil tip.

Centuries of publicity have left most gardeners with the impression that daffodils are always "harbingers of spring." However, did you know that there are at least four *Narcissus* species in southern Europe and northern Africa that do not start flowering until autumn? These flowers appear to exploit insects that do not even emerge until late in the season. A number of botanists have commented on how the fragrance of the green-flowered narcissus *(N. viridiflorus)* seems to become stronger as the sun sets. It appears to be pollinated by sphinx moths.

John Blanchard, one of England's greatest living authorities on the wild species of daffodils, shreds the sentimental notion of daffodils as flowers restricted to springtime. He insists that, around the Mediterranean basin, he has seen different *Narcissus* species in bloom in every month but August.

In an earlier chapter I suggested that the evolution of floral tubes encouraged the formation of the breeding system Charles Darwin called heterostyly. Recent work by a trio of scientists from New Zealand and Israel has proven that both angel's tears *(N. triandrus)* and *N. fernandesii* get up to much the same pin and thrum tricks usually associated with primroses and wood sorrels.

Delving into floral structure now allows us to answer the big question: What is the difference between a true daffodil and a narcissus or jonquil? Some purists continue to insist that only the subspecies of *N. pseudonarcissus* found in Britain is the real daff. That's ridiculous. It's true that this plant is a "parent" of many garden varieties (including the much loved King Alfred). On the other hand, at least six of the *Narcissus* species native to southern Europe and the Middle East have also been crossed repeatedly to form new breeds marketed as official daffodils.

It's easiest to say that *all* daffodils are narcissi but not *all* narcissi are daffodils. A daffodil must have two features. First, its stalk always ends in a solitary flower. That automatically excludes plants like the paper whites *(N. papyraceous)*, angel's tears, and poet's narcissus, as they bunch many small flowers at the stalk's tip. Second, the flower's corona must be longer than it is wide. In fact, the corona should be as long, or longer than, the loose tepals. That means we must also exclude the jonquils *(N. jonquila)* and hoop petticoats *(N. bulbocodium)*, even though their stalks end in a single flower. The corona must form an extended trumpet, not a broad, shallow cup. Although the wild daffodil of Britain passes both tests, so does the cyclamen-flowered narcissus, the small wild daffodil *(N. minor)*, the Asturian daffodil *(N. asturiensis)*, and another two or three species that tend to lack distinctive common names.

The real sign that a plant has become a garden favorite lies in the range of varieties available to both the amateur gardener and the obsessive connoisseur. Frankly, I find that much of the history of flower breeding is a rather dull affair in which horticulturists make very different plants all look the same. There seems to be a parallel trend to select forms in which the number of petals can be increased until the blossom is turned into a featureless ball with the extra petals concealing the "naughty" sexual organs like extra layers of lace underpants. When they are mixed together in a vase it's

Angel's tears *(N. triandrus)* is not a true daffodil. Its stalk ends in more than one flower, and the nodding, bell corona of each blossom is about as long as it is wide. These flowers employ a pin and thrum system. PHOTO BY P. E. BRANDHAM

often difficult to distinguish among multipetaled peonies versus roses versus camellias versus magnolias, etc. That's why double daffs were called rose daffodils or bulroses before the 1600s. I have seen a copy of a watercolor of these flowers by Pieter van Kouwenhoorn that must have been painted before 1650.

Despite an early European interest in daffodil breeding, there wasn't much to choose from until quite recently. A century ago there were fewer than thirty registered cultivars of *Narcissus.* As we approach the end of this century, the American Daffodil Society has registered over ten thousand varieties worldwide! Even the Japanese have turned a very serious eye to daffodil breeding. What happened?

While you can cross two very different daffodils and make healthy hybrids, both sets of the parents' chromosomes often fail to recombine in the cells of the hybrid seeds. If each parent daff has fourteen chromosomes, their offspring may have twenty-eight. About 75 percent of all cultivated daffodils have twice the number of chromosomes as their parents. It's also possible to cross a daff that has fourteen chromosomes with a species that has twenty and end up with offspring that have seventeen chromosomes.

Some garden varieties of daffodils now have up to four times the number of chromosomes found in their wild ancestors. This form of chromosome evolution is called polyploidy. It occurs naturally enough in many wild plants, including some *Narcissus* species, as well as strawberries, ferns, and saltmarsh grass *(Spartina).* This time, though, man's tinkering with daffs has hurried the sort of genetic explosion that usually takes thousands, perhaps millions of years when different populations of plants exchange chromosomes without human interference.

The more chromosomes each new daff generation acquires the more likely "accidents" will occur as chromosomes separate and divide while the flower prepares sperm and egg cells.

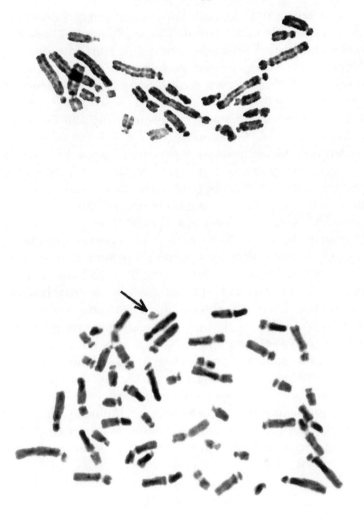

Above. Wild paperwhite narcissus has only twenty-two chromosomes in each cell.

Below. Killara is a cultivated form with forty-five chromosomes and a *beta* fragment *(arrow)* in each cell. Killara had a paperwhite ancestor but also descends from hybrids between such garden breeds as Empress and Grand Monarch. PHOTO BY P. E. BRANDHAM

Some breeds carry additional chunks of broken chromosomes known as *betas*. In other daffs the "arms" of dividing chromosomes have joined together turning two pairs into one big chromosome. There are hybrids sporting a whole extra chromosome, following errors in cell division. It's this sort of messy coupling that results in cultivars like Highfield Beauty with thirty-one, or Killara with both forty-five and *beta* fragments.

Can you imagine how this bewildering hash of DNA keeps changing the appearance of daffodils with each generation? The effect of one gene may be either lost entirely, *or* duplicated many times over, *or* even become suppressed by the combined effect of a different cluster of genes. This may ultimately affect such features as growth rate and flowering time, flower color and size, corona shape and fragrance.

I thought I'd finally enjoy a respite from daffodils, at least for a couple of years, by trading St. Louis for Sydney. Instead, I arrived in a city in which daff season lasts almost five months. Walk by any local flower stall between June and October and the bouquets of narcissi knock you over with their combined scent. The climate is much milder here, so more of the heat-loving varieties from the Mediterranean can be grown throughout Australia's southeast.

Can you keep a secret? I'm actually beginning to, uh . . . like daffodils again. In another month we'll take a weekend away from Sydney and look for hoop petticoats in the gardens of the Blue Mountains.

CHAPTER 14

Orchids in a Cemetery

Let me slumber in the hollow where the wattle
    blossoms wave,
  With never stone or rail to fence my bed;
Should the sturdy station children pull the bush
    flowers on my grave,
  I may chance to hear them romping overhead.

Adam Lindsay Gordon, "The Sick Stockrider"

On sunny spring days I like to haunt the rural cemeteries of southern Australia. My motives are scientific, since old graveyards are often rich in wildflowers. Decades ago, the surrounding countryside may have been ploughed under for wheat or trampled by generations of sheep, but within the barbed wire of the cemetery fence the original heath or grassland habitats survive.

And not just any cemetery will do. The prospect of finding wildflowers depends on the history of the burial societies that established and maintained the first plots. If a wealthy farming community grew up around the site, you can forget about finding wildflowers now. Residents demanded perpetual care for their loved ones and copied the cemeteries of the Northern Hemisphere. The bushland was replaced by lawns of European grasses and "mournful trees" like yews and willows.

Any Australian plants persisting were sprayed into oblivion with the coming of modern herbicides.

The best cemeteries, from a flower-watcher's viewpoint, are those associated with sleepier communities, where residents have remained few and far between. Shires associated with gold-prospecting during the last century are often most promising. Broken dreams meant that burial societies lacked funds to afford more respectable conventions. At best, someone was appointed to keep the vegetation mowed. This checked the spindly and woody growth of young eucalypts, wattles, and ti-tree *(Leptospermum)*, but it benefited perennial herbs. Most Australian herbs can't form dense, vivid populations where trees and spreading shrubs outcompete them for available sunlight.

Consequently, some country graveyards have become important refuges for vulnerable wildflowers as man has taken bigger bites out of local environments. Plant geographers head for Australian cemeteries to find some of the largest populations of kangaroo paws *(Anigozanthos* spp.) and some endangered members of the daisy family such as the button wrinklewort *(Rutidosis leptorrhynchoides)*. I look for orchids behind the tombstones.

There are about five hundred species of orchids native to Australia. As you travel along the coast south of the Tropic of Capricorn, the orchids that cling to tree branches or boulders quickly decline in number and variety. The most southerly corners of this continent lie within warm-temperate or wet-Mediterranean zones. Therefore, more than half of the orchid species in Australia grow in true, albeit shallow, soils. Most of these ground orchids endure the hottest months, and even the stress of drought *years*, by retreating to their underground storage organs, known as root-stem tuberoids.

Root-stem tuberoids combine tissue and developmental characteristics of both true stems and roots. They are odd little organs, as each tuberoid resembles an unequal pair of testicles; hence the word *orchid* (Greek *orchis* means testicle). Each "testicle" is really a storage bag filled primarily with carbohydrates used during alternating periods of growth and dormancy. During each normal season of growth one testicle seems to shrink as its starches are digested and transferred to elongating shoots. Meanwhile, the second testicle starts to plump up as new leaves make food and send sugar molecules underground for storage in the second testicle. Tuberoid structure and function seems unique to the orchid family, but it is not unique to Australia and is regularly employed by many species of ground orchids throughout the world.

Some Australian orchids can reproduce without seed by manufacturing daughter or replacement tuberoids. A lone plant can turn into a colony of clones over the years, since a healthy adult may produce one or more underground stalks (stolons) toward the end of each growth cycle. The tip of each stalk swells up to form a new, self-planted tuberoid. That's why some species of sun orchids *(Thelymitra)* always seem to grow in tight tufts, and some bird orchids *(Chiloglottis)* form closely knit zigzags across the heathland.

The aborigines dug up the tuberoids of some species and ate them after roasting them like little potatoes. European settlers fancied the colors and bizarre shapes of such flowers, although most ground orchids offer blooms less than an inch in width. The popular names of the most common orchids often changed from region to region. For example, *Pterostylis nutans* was one of the first Australian orchids I ever collected. I found them in a reserve in Victoria back in 1978, but the same species forms lush patches throughout much of south-eastern Australia. My Victorian coworkers said it was a nodding greenhood. Had I found it first in New South Wales I might have been told it was a parrot's-beak orchid. Do Tasmanians still call it cow-horns?

What is it about the British tradition that encourages both

scientists and colonists to give descriptive names to the most unfamiliar flowers? Back in 1803, George Caley (a botanist explorer working for Sir Joseph Banks at Kyew) found *Pterostylis nutans* in what today is a busy suburb of Sydney. He became obsessed with discovering new species of the hooded orchids he called Druid's Caps. It's a shame this name never stuck.

When you read the old accounts of people sent off to teach children living way off in "the bush" or listen to interviews with retired schoolteachers, there is a familiar story. Their students were taken on botany walks and taught the names of wildflowers. This was treated as an exercise to train young memories that would soon be required to memorize historical dates and long poems. If a teacher found a flower that was not immediately identifiable, the class was invited to "make up a new name." No wonder common names vary with the territory.

The early colonists seem to have passed all their tests in creative naming. Only a few species of Australian orchids have names copying their distant relations in Britain. Children seem to have resisted naming wild orchids after the cultivated flowers their parents or grandparents brought over to brighten homesteads. *Diuris* species are partial exceptions to the rule, as their flowers have such a bright sheen and extravagant blotches that some species were christened after garden favorites and may be addressed as purple pansies *(D. longifolia)*, wallflower orchids *(D. corymbosa)*, golden cowslips *(D. behria)*, and buttercup doubletails *(D. aequalis)*. We will see, though, that the peculiar shapes of *Diuris* flowers have encouraged much more imaginative names, and the orchid's sex life offers a key to its "secret identity."

Southern Australia enjoys such mild climates you can find different orchids in bloom each season. To describe them all would require another book. Let's observe the plants from late winter until the end of spring, as this is when orchid

diversity peaks. We'll stick to the orchids John Kelly first intro-
duced me to in the remnant woodlands around the Hard
Hills of St. Arnaud and the old cemetery in the shire of Kara
Kara, Victoria (northeast of Melbourne). You'll excuse me if
I enjoy an author's license and also wander a bit through the
Blue Mountains of New South Wales. Each common name
tells a story about the function of floral morphology and
color.

The first big flush of ground orchids occurs during the last
month of winter. August tends to be cloudy and the orchids
have modest colors of green and brown with whitish streaks.
It's easy to miss them against the litter of twigs and leaves.
This is a damp time of year when mushrooms appear. These
fungi are the food of the maggots born of tiny swarms of
fungus gnats (Mycetophilidae). Adult gnats swarm to mate
and the females lay their eggs in the soft flesh of the mushrooms. The ground orchids of late winter and early spring
exploit this seasonal cycle.

Mosquito orchids (*Acianthus* supp.) are small plants, but
they seem to be among the most adaptable of all Australian
ground orchids. They'll form colonies in forest clearings or in
cemetery plots. They even survive in sheep pastures, provided
they grow up against the fence stakes where browsers can't
reach them. When the flower expands, a droplet of nectar
appears at the base of the lip petal and this nourishes the
adult gnats that carry off the wads of orchid pollen on their
backs. The forms of mosquito orchids must be admired with
a hand lens, but the dead-horse orchid *(A. caudatus)* has
rather extravant organs for such a tiny flower. Its three sepals
are long, purple, and threadlike. You really can imagine it
resembles a racehorse on its back. Naturalists note the offen-
sive carrion-*cum*-compost-heap odor that is supposed to be
attractive to gnats.

The helmet orchids *(Corybas)* are among the least conspicuous of winter flowers. When they bloom, each iodine-stained flower tends to be almost flush with the ground, and most species seem to prefer the shadiest sites, often hiding under shrubs or in mossy hummocks in slow-draining gullies. The floral sculpture is impressive, as a wide sepal clasps the curved, scalloped lip petal turning the flower into a miniature version of the ornate trumpet on an antique gramophone. Their floral biology has received little study, but observations of the toothed helmet orchid *(C. diemenicus)* suggest these trumpets mimic the gilled interior of a mushroom. A pregnant gnat crawls down the lip and lays her eggs. On her way out she contacts the sexual organs and carries off pollen globs. Of course, when the maggots hatch, they probably starve to death.

Over a hundred species of greenhoods *(Pterostylis)* are found exclusively in Australia, with the majority native to the southeastern corner. Their beaky, juglike flowers usually come equipped with two sepal tips that have been transformed into a Martian's antennae. It's almost impossible to confuse them with any other orchid, and in my opinion they are the real harbingers of the coming Australian spring. With so many different greenhoods, some species show a fine capacity to recolonize land damaged by man's greed. My friend John Kelly took me to a favorite place in the Hard Hills, the site where prospectors had drawn water from the creek, probably with a horsepower-turned drum, to separate alluvial gold from rock. The great doughnut-shaped depression in the ground was filled with dwarf greenhoods *(P. nana)*.

The pollination system of some greenhoods can turn a male gnat into a literal "prisoner of love." The male gnat enters the greenhood's jug through a narrow "spout" formed by the curved hood and the lower plate of sepals. The lip petal of the flowers of nodding greenhoods, rusty hoods *(P. rufa)*, baggy britches *(P. vittata)*, etc., wear a dark, pimply stalk, or callous, often plumed or encircled with fine hairs. The male

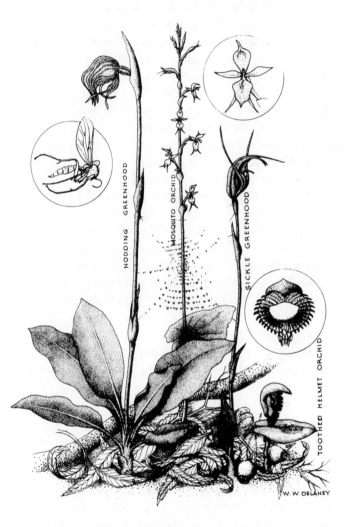

The greenhoods *(Pterostylis)*, mosquito orchids *(Acianthus)*, and helmet orchids of late winter–early spring often bloom in moist, shady spots. All appear to be dependent on fungus gnats *(Mycomya)* for cross-pollination.
ILLUSTRATION BY W. W. DELANEY

gnat mistakes this dummy for a female gnat and attempts to mate with it. The lip is hinged, cocked, and very sensitive to slight pressure. The weight of the gnat triggers the lip petal, which is jolted upward slamming the insect into the tip of the sexual organs. When the lip relaxes after a few minutes, the groggy gnat crawls out of the spout, bearing the brittle pollinia on his back. You can trigger this trap mechanism with a bit of straw and it snaps up within less than a second. Gnats don't seem to learn much from their experience with bondage, and cross-pollination occurs when males repeat their amorous adventures in a second flower.

As the spring days become longer and brighter, most of the gnat exploiters retire. They will be replaced by orchids with larger flowers that open wide and do not, as a rule, form chambered helmets or hoods. Most of these early- to mid-spring species come in delightful hues, for this is the time of year when cemeteries and heaths are transformed by blue, pink, yellow, and indigo petals. The remaining orchids dress flowers in rather funereal shades almost bordering on the black. Regardless of color, virtually all the species in bloom now are designed to deceive their pollinators, and they fool insects far larger than fungus gnats. Color, presentation, and scent determine whether each species fools its "mark" with empty promises of food *or* sex.

The more than seventy *Caladenia* species show how a closely related group of plants can specialize in mimicry. The short petals of about thirty species display pretty "Easter egg" or bronze colors and have fragrances reminiscent of perfumed bath soaps, jam, or musk. No wonder they are known as fairy orchids. Their lip petals are short, starched aprons usually ornamented with loose stalks (calli) tipped white, yellow, or purple. Children call such stalks fairy fingers. Fairy orchids attract hover flies (syrphids) or small bees collecting food for their offspring. The colorful stalks may look and smell like stamens stuffed with pollen grains but they are sterile structures yielding no reward no matter how hard they are sucked or scraped. Pollinia are deposited on the insect's back once it abandons the calli stalks on the lip petal.

In contrast, the remaining *Caladenia* species seem mottled with rust and glossy, deep-maroon tones. The tips of floral segments tend to narrow into exquisitely fine tails releasing an odor no human nose can detect but is so compelling to pollinators. The lip petal is often a wide, hinged comb. Dainty fingers have been replaced by gross, blackened knobs that cluster together, forming a pattern like the body of an insect. These broad flowers jiggle and bob in the spring breeze and are known as spider orchids. Tiphiid wasps pounce on the fake insect on each lip petal. At one time, some naturalists thought spider orchids were mimicking real spiders, and the wasps pollinated the orchid while stinging their "false prey." However, all the tiphiids caught on spider orchids have turned out to be males. The knobs on the lip petal comprise a dummy female and the odor of the spider orchid acts as a sort of wasp aphrodisiac. Perhaps it's fortunate we can't smell it.

Male tiphiids are "tricked" by other spring orchids that are closely related to spider caladenias. This includes both the bird *(Chiloglottis)* and elbow orchids *(Arthrochilus)*. Look for the dark, chunky sculptures on their lip petals. Some flowers lure quite a broad range of tiphiids. Other plants may have evolved systems in which all male wasps attracted belong to the same genus.

Some food mimics also appear to carry on a rather specialized line of deceit. In the last century the correspondence of botanists and collectors often remarked on how *Diruis* orchids resembled the lilac, orange, and yellow flowers on the bushes of parrot peas and bacon-and-egg peas. The pea blossoms may have reddish brown or purple splotches but so do the orchids. The lip petal of the orchid is folded so it mimics the lower, ridged keel petal of the pea blossom. The orchid

By mid-spring the orchids divide into two groups. Food mimics like pink fairies *(Caladenia latifolia)* and scented sun orchids *(Thelymitra nuda)* lure hungry bees and wasps. In contrast, beardies *(Calochilus)*, green combs *(Caladenia dilatata)*, and bird orchids *(Chiloglottis)* are sex mimics with lip petals simulating the bodies of female wasps. ILLUSTRATION BY W. W. DELANEY

flower has pushed back its wide, flattened lateral petals and merged them with the broad dorsal sepal. This would seem to copy the banner petal of the pea blossom that normally attracts the attention of flying insects.

Observations completed only a decade ago show that *Diuris* flowers deceive native bees that drink pea nectar in spring and feed their young on pea pollen. It's the earlike or winglike petals of the orchid that give some species beloved names like donkey orchid *(D. corymbosa)*, nanny goat *(D. laevis)*, golden moths *(D. lanceolata)*, and cat's face *(D. filifolia)*.

The sun orchids *(Thelymitra)* are personal favorites. They really *are* flowers of the sun requiring cloudless mornings, when the temperature rises above seventy degrees, before they open wide. I have seen the cemetery in Kara Kara turn blue with thousands of flowers of slender sun orchid *(T. pauciflora)* and scented sun orchid *(T. nuda)*. For some unknown reason, most flowers in the orchid family rarely paint themselves blue. However, more than half of the thirty to forty species of sun orchids range from a dull, bluish slate to a glowing azure.

Wildflower artist and conservationist Kathleen McArthur shares my appreciation for these plants, and she lives in Australia's tropical north where they are far less common. She has written: "It is not always the species making the biggest splash of color that one thinks of first. It may be just one or two blue scented sun orchids, so rare and sweet they bring September to mind."

In fact, there must be at least one species of sun orchid for each band of the rainbow, and one rare species *(T. epipactoides)* offers blue-green *or* bronze-tinted petals. The cemetery in Kara Kara also offers flowering species of sun orchids in pink, red-orange, yellow, and purple. Their scents often have a nostalgic quality that's hard to pin down. Some fans of the lemon orchid *(T. antennifera)* insist that, when it is massed, there really is a characteristic odor of citrus peel; others are

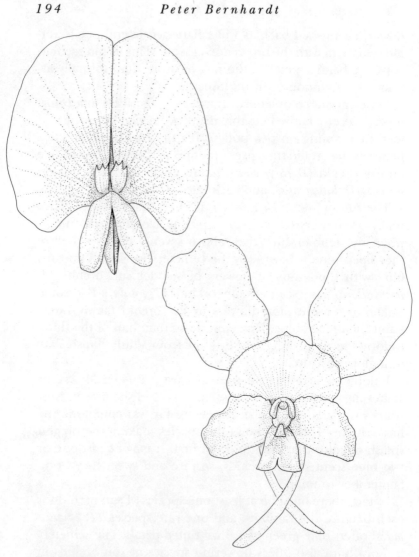

Food mimic orchids can be specialized "copycats."
Left. Native bees often depend on the scented, colorful flowers of native peas for nectar.
Right. A twintail or donkey ear orchid *(Diuris)* is scented and colorful, takes a "pea blossom shape," but offers no nectar. ILLUSTRATION BY J. MYERS

Left. In contrast, the tiny flowers of sallow wattle *(A. longifolia)* are packed into long spikes. The stems are leafless and the flat green foliage consists of modified, flattened branches (phyllodes). PHOTO BY TREVOR HAWKESWOOD

Below. Lycaste bradeorum is from South America and has a bucketlike lip petal. Yellow nymphs tend to produce the spiciest scents reminiscent of cloves. PHOTO BY R. DRESSLER

Left. Most magnolias of North America release their seeds each autumn. Ripe ovaries in the same cluster split open; red seeds drop out, each dangling by a thread until plucked off by a migrating bird. PHOTO BY RICHARD B. FIGLAR

Below. The Australian orchids of later winter (August) tend to be drably colored as they wait for fungus gnats. The petals of helmet orchids like *Corybas dilatatus* may have a moist, clammy feel and may smell a bit like chopped mushrooms. PHOTO BY ARTHUR WELLS

reminded of vanilla extract. I find that they smell like old breeds of garden roses.

A sun orchid flower lacks a distinctive lip petal. Its lip petal is usually the same shape and color as the two lateral petals and may even be indistinguishable from the three outer sepals. This is a very rare condition within the orchid family. Pollinating insects do not use the lip of a sun orchid as a landing platform or as a place to look for food; they land on the tip of the sexual organs (the column) instead. The column wears a hood of sterile, fused stamens decorated with little teeth, brushes, or horns. Once again, bees and flies mistake these sculptures for real pollen. As the insect bashes away at the false reward, it brushes against a sticky gland (the viscidium) that glues the hidden pollinia to its head or abdomen. Bees leave the fringed columns of the leopard orchid *(T. fuscolutea)* with balls of pollen glued to their little banded butts!

Close cousins of the sun orchids are sex mimics, but you wouldn't recognize the dummy female . . . not immediately. While I was exploring a reserve with Bill Delaney (who has contributed so many illustrations to this book), he pointed a finger at the ground and said, "Look, Peter, a bearded Bolshie!" Yes, there was a face in this flower—an *agent provocateur* with a sepal cap pulled over his face, a big nose, two beady eyes, and a thick, bushy beard (like the portraits of Karl Marx). These flowers are also known more affectionately as beardies, brown beards, or old-man orchids *(Calochilus),* and the lip petal mimics the hairy abdomen of female scoliid wasps. The fake eyes (not present in all species) are located on a special collar under the noselike column.

Orchids that deceive bees, wasps, and large flies are so successful that different species overlap and continue their bewildering displays until early autumn, when the white sepals of the parson's bands *(Eriochilus cuccullatus)* pop up on the burial mounds in the Kara Kara cemetery. By the last month of spring, though, these deceivers will be infiltrated by another group of noncomformists that actually offer nectar. These latecomers cluster many flower buds on each erect stalk. A few buds open on each stalk every day, starting from the bottom and working upward. The open flowers have shapes like short tubes or shallow bowls holding nectar droplets.

Don't be put off by names like leek orchids *(Prasophyllum)* or onion orchids *(Microtis)*. For a change, the common names reflect how the orchid's leaves resemble miniature versions of the greenery of an onion or leek. In fact, most naturalists agree that many of these orchids have sweet perfumes like a lily-of-the-valley. Sometimes they feed a most unexpected clientele.

Onion orchids are not much to look at but some species are hardy, forming tufts in cemeteries, and I've even found them in some really awful waste places where the original vegetation has vanished. The nectar in the short flowers attracts quite a number of small flying insects, but the slender onion orchid *(M. parviflora)* is one of the few plants on this planet pollinated consistently by worker ants. I have watched the ants *(Idiomyrmex* spp.) running quickly up and down the orchid stalks investigating the narrow, greenish flowers. The pollinia adheres to their heads and looks like crumbly yellow pompoms.

Prasophyllum species wear their lip petals pointing upward (nonresupinate) like ruffled hankies sticking out of jacket pockets, but their columns hang upside down. The eighty or so species can be divided roughly in half. The midge orchids have nodding flowers the size of pinheads, and their lip petals are often fringed like an eyelash. Some taxonomists think they deserve their own genus *(Genoplesium)*. True leek orchids hold their blossoms horizontally and lack hairy fringes. You don't need a magnifying glass to appreciate the beauty of

Midge, leek *(Prasophyllum)*, and onion orchids *(Microtis)* bloom by late spring crowding many small flowers onto the same stem. Each flower makes some nectar feeding a wide variety of insects. Onion orchids seem particularly attractive to thirsty ants depositing their pollen wads just above the worker's jaws. ILLUSTRATION BY W. W. DELANEY

these bouquets, for individual flowers are often as wide as a pinkie nail and may have gaudy contrasting stripes.

Leek orchids have sweet odors and are pollinated by a combination of thirsty hover flies, wasps, and bees. Midge orchids tend to be a drab brownish green, but they can have a powerful smell like overripe fruit attracting eager vinegar and fruit flies (drosophilids).

Last comes the austral ladies' tresses *(Spiranthes sinensis)*. Ladies' tresses is one of the few common names for an orchid uniting Australians and New Zealanders with Canadians, Americans, and Brits . . . and why not? Most of the world's forty-two *Spiranthes* species are confined to the Northern Hemisphere. The name Austral ladies's tress is a bit of a misnomer, since *S. sinensis* has one of the widest distributions, flaunting its pink and white flowers as far north as Siberia, through the Himalayas and the mountains of Malaysia too! The antipodes simply represents this flexible orchid's most southerly address.

Their short, tubular flowers form a spiral up the stalk, like a woman's braided tresses. Some of these flowers bloom on through the heat of late December. Solitary bees, commercial honeybees, and the meadow argus butterfly *(Precis villida calybe)* have all been recorded as visiting these orchids for more than sixty years. In exchange for a cup of Christmas cheer, the flower fixes its pollinia at the base of each insect's mouthparts.

Will Australian cemeteries continue to act as wildflower refuges? Some rural graveyards have shown some disturbing trends. The bereaved are placing large concrete slabs on top of the remains of their loved ones. No ground orchid will ever grow on top of that. If a cemetery of only a few acres becomes crowded with such monuments, the wildflowers will be pushed into narrower margins of survival.

When the Australian artist Clifton Pugh died a couple of years ago, his family received permission to bury him on his property in his favorite orchid reserve. The vegetation was carefully removed unharmed, like segments of a thick rug. It was replaced with the same loving care after the body had been buried. Spider orchids bloom on Pugh's grave each spring. This seems to be the finest tribute to one who loved the bush in life. Are there better ways to spend eternity than in the embrace of orchids?

Annotated Bibliography

CHAPTER 1: MUSE UNDER GLASS

*Atwood, J. "Pollination of *Paphiopedilum rothschildianum:* Brood-site Deception." *National Geographic Research,* Spring 1985: pp. 247–254. The tables are easy to follow and the text avoids much of the terminology that alienates so many amateur botanists. Truth is not stranger than fiction, but is much more interesting to the scientist.

*Primack, R. B. "Longevity of Individual Flowers." *Annual Review of Ecology and Systematics* 16 (1985): pp. 15–38. Greenhouses extend the life of individual flowers as zoos may extend the lives of animals. Tests and field records indicate that the limits of floral lifespan may be genetically set, reflecting variations in breeding systems, the predictability of the plant's environment, flower size, and class of pollinators.

Shattuck, R. "Object Lesson for Modern Art." *Henri Rousseau: Essays by Roger Shattuck, Henri Béhar, Michel Hoog, Carolyn Lanchner and William Rubin.* New York: The Museum of Modern Art, 1985. Shattuck's evidence turns most of the anecdotes surrounding Rousseau's life into sheer myth. The book is actually a catalog of a Rousseau exhibition held at the museum in 1984–85, and includes the majority of the artist's most important works.

*Denotes scientific literature that is probably unavailable in most public libraries. Readers are encouraged to look in the libraries of botanical gardens and arboreta, natural history museums, and any university or college with its own department of biology or botany.

Woods, May, and Warren Arete. *Glasshouses: A History of Greenhouses, Orangeries and Conservatories.* New York: Rizzoli/Aurum, 1988. Begins with the orangeries of royalty and ends with our current fad for glazed swimming pools. It's a popular history, yet the subject matter has been researched thoroughly and is presented concisely. An added benefit is that illustrations and quotes indicate the wide range of poets, architects, and painters contributing to the appreciation of the greenhouse.

CHAPTER 2: A SANCTUARY FOR THE DREAMTIME

Duncan, B. D., and G. Isaac. *Ferns and Allied Plants of Victoria, Tasmania and South Australia.* Melbourne: Melbourne University Press, 1986. This will give the reader a much clearer impression of the plants that ornament or frame Ricketts's work and are distributed through the Dandenongs.

Seddon, G. "Cuddlepie and Other Surrogates." *Westerly* 2 (1988): pp. 143–155. A differing opinion is always useful. Seddon visited the William Ricketts Sanctuary and admired the artist's convictions while dismissing most of Billy's work.

CHAPTER 3: SEVEN FAMILIES IN ONE SALAD

Anderson, E. *Plants, Man and Life.* Berkeley: University of California Press, 1952. A popular treatment of the science of ethnobotany written by one of America's greatest botanists. Anderson clarified the role of hybridization in plant evolution and stimulated generations of students by weaving together information about plant domestication based on Soviet, British, and American theories.

Heywood, V. H., consulting editor. *Flowering Plant Families of the World.* London: Oxford University Press, 1978. Taxonomists are not in complete agreement as to the exact number of families and where certain families "stop" and others begin. Heywood's treatment is too conservative for some, but the large illustrations are easy to understand and the text avoids a lot of terminology that often makes such books inaccessible to laypersons.

Raven, Peter H., Ray F. Evert, and Susan E. Eichhorn. *Biology of Plants, Fourth Edition.* New York: Worth, 1986. Written proof that a textbook for college students needn't be dense and dry. Chapter 20 provides a concise description of the cells making up all plant tissues, while Chapter 30 discusses how different cultures exploit plant products.

de Rougemont, G. M. *A Field Guide to the Crops of Britain and Europe.* London: William Collins, 1989. Few of us go to Europe to watch "veggies." Nevertheless, this is the most recent popular treatment of cultivated plants on the Continent, and the author integrates plant biology with human history.

CHAPTER 4: CROCUS HOCUS-POCUS

Bowles, E. A. *A Handbook of Crocus and Colchicum for Gardeners.* London: The Bodley Head, 1952 (revised edition). Even professional botanists continue to return to Bowles for aspects of crocus lore, growing tips, and diseases. Bowles discusses both crocus hybrids and poisonous colchicums with the enthusiasm of a wine buff comparing vintages.

*Chichiricco, G., and M. G. Caiola. "*Crocus sativus* Pollen Tube Growth in Intra- and Interspecific Pollination." *Caryologia* 37 (1984): pp. 115–125. Fluorescence microscopy becomes a modern yet simple tool (I use it all the time) to help determine when and why plants may suffer sexual breakdowns.

Evans, A. *The Palace of Minos.* London: Macmillan, 1921–1935. Yes, there are far more recent works interpreting the excavations of ancient Crete but these four thick volumes are still impressive and informative. Evans seems to have described every item that emerged from the layers of the dig.

*Mathew, B. "*Crocus sativus* and Its Allies (Iridaceae)." *Plant Systematics and Evolution* 128 (1977): pp. 89–103. The author is an employee of the Royal Botanic Gardens, Kew. England's Kew gardens remains the world center for crocus collections. Descriptions and distributions of those autumn-flowering species, most often confused with commercial saffron, are provided.

CHAPTER 5: THE PASSIONATE DESSERT

*Bailey, L. H. *The Standard Cyclopedia of Horticulture,* Volume III—P–Z. New York: Macmillan, 1942. It's worthwhile searching for this reprint of the original edition, as it contains a wealth of passionflower folklore, descriptions of prized breeds, and fine old illustrations. I'm not knocking the modern revisions of this essential book, but each new version must be heavily edited to make room for new entries.

*Gilbert, Lawrence E., and Peter Raven, editors. *Coevolution of Animals and Plants*. Austin: University of Texas Press, 1975. Contains a long chapter by Gilbert (pp. 210–240) on butterfly-vine connections, showing it's a ménage à trois. The caterpillars prey mercilessly on the passion vines, but the adults are pollinators of the flowers of tropical members of the cucumber family.

*National Research Council: Ad Hoc Panel of the Advisory Committee on Technology Innovation Board on Science and Technology for International Development. *Lost Crops of the Incas*. Washington: National Academy Press, 1989. The Andes have been the birthplace of many useful plants we now take for granted. The panel explores the potential of ten *Passiflora* species and insists that soft-drink industries are investing heavily in passion-fruit culture.

Symons, Michael. *One Continuous Picnic: A History of Eating in Australia*. Adelaide: Duck Press, 1981. How does a young country acquire its cuisine? Comments on Australian food and eating habits, made by foreigners, season a lighthearted history. Symons is provocative when he calls the pavlova "Depression food," as its appearance around 1935 appealed to escapist fantasies weary of ground meat, condensed milk, and porridge.

CHAPTER 6: THRILLED BY THRUMS

*Bernhardt, P. "Pollination Ecology of *Oxalis violacea* (Oxalidaceae) Following a Controlled Grass Fire." *Plant Systematics and Evolution* 171 (1990): pp. 147–155. Presents the ratio and reproductive rates of pins versus thrums, and the native bees involved in the transfer of pollen from one form to the other.

*Denton, Melinda F. "A Monograph of *Oxalis* Section *Ionoxalis* (Oxalidaceae) in North America." *Publications of the Museum, Michigan State University* 4 (1973): pp. 459–615. Monographs may seem a bit dry and specialized, but we need them to obtain a clearer idea of the range of diversity in nature. Denton treats only the pink and purple wood sorrels, but they offer plenty of variation in breeding forms.

Duthie, Ruth. *Florists' Flowers and Societies.* Great Britain: Thomas (Haverfordwest), 1988. A brief but absorbing account of those flowers bred for competition in Britain. The concise, witty text pays special attention to the history of primrose and auricula "improvements."

*Richards, A. J. *Plant Breeding Systems.* London: George Allen and Unwin, 1986. Heterostylous flowers receive their own chapter, and the author concentrates on the "gene play" behind the flower forms.

CHAPTER 7: SOMETHING WITH POISON IN IT

*Bentley, Barbara, and Thomas Elias, editors. *The Biology of Nectaries.* New York: Columbia University Press, 1983. There are eight contributions written by twelve scientists on topics ranging from the importance of nectar in agricultural crops to how animals steal nectar from inaccessible flowers. The Bakers wrote a short but rigorous history about how and when different substances in nectar were discovered.

*Fahn, A. *Secretory Tissues in Plants.* London: Academic Press, 1979. Dr. Fahn is regarded as one of the great pioneers studying the anatomy and tissues of plant glands. Not only will the reader learn about the nectaries, but there is ample information on how quite different cells secrete water, salt, glue, and fragrances. There are chapters on the weaponry of stinging hairs and the "tentacles" of carnivorous plants.

*Lorch, Jacob. "The Discovery of Nectar and Nectaries and Its Relation to Views on Flowers and Insects." *Isis* 69 (1978): pp. 514–533. A paper on one of the slowest discoveries in botanical history proves to be wickedly entertaining. Men who fancied themselves "natural philosophers" (including Goethe and Rousseau) sneered at their coworkers, but then "couldn't see the forest for the bees." It's amazing how glandular bumps in a flower have played such a long, large role influencing how scientists choose to define reality.

CHAPTER 8: THE HOON'S NEST

Hardin, G. J., editor. *Flora of New South Wales.* Volumes I and II. Kensington: New South Wales University Press, 1990–91. By the time you read this line it's possible that the last two volumes of *Flora of N.S.W.* will also be available. English descriptions and diagnostic keys combine with inked illustrations and color photographs, providing a definitive introduction to over six thousand species in Australia's oldest state. The flora of the area is so diverse because its borders stretch from Old World rain forest to inland desert.

*Small, E., and A. Cronquist. "A Practical and Natural Taxonomy for *Cannabis.*" *Taxon* 25 (1976): pp. 405–435. Two scientists agreed to combine their independent efforts to produce what I feel is the most convincing interpretation of variation in marijuana. Black-and-white photographs of hard *Cannabis* fruits show how weeds may differ from crop plants. The authors provide a key to identifying subspecies and varieties (provided you are prepared to extract the cannabinoid resins yourself).

CHAPTER 9: WATTLES FOR THE EMPRESS

Costermans, L. *Native Trees and Shrubs of Southeastern Australia.* Adelaide, Australia: Rigby, 1983. One of the finest, clearest contributions to the study of the woody plants of a region that I have ever read. The section on *Acacia* is carefully illustrated and makes a confusing group accessible.

*Ducker, S. C., and R. B. Knox. "The Australian History of *Acacia* Miller and Its Pollen." In *Pollination '82,* edited by E. G. Williams, R. B. Knox, J. H. Gilbert, and P. Bernhardt. Melbourne: University of Melbourne, 1982. Jumps from the Middle Eastern acacias that may have played the role of the burning bush to the "Age of Reason," when Australian acacias made their debut in Europe.

Lamb, C. "Knight to Empress." *The Garden,* February 1991: pp. 71–75. Sir Joseph Banks and Empress Joséphine had much in common, including a botanical artist, many scientists, and lots of rare plants. Banks believed that the sciences were never at war.

*Stirton, C. H., and J. L. Zarucchi, editors. *Advances in Legume Biology. Monographs in Systematic Botany from The Missouri Botanical Garden, Number 29.* St. Louis: The Missouri Botanical Garden, 1989. Fifty-four scientists write about different aspects of the life-cycles of the plant family, including all the true peas, beans, and acacias, for nearly eight hundred and fifty pages. An index points the way to *Acacia* studies by analyzing the architecture of their trees and flowering branches, development and construction of flower buds and seeds, interactions between their pollen and pistils, dependency on their pollinators, and how they are attacked by insects.

CHAPTER 10: WHITE NUN/YELLOW NYMPH

*Fowlie, J. A. *The Genus Lycaste.* Pomona, CA: Day Printing, 1970. The most recent treatment of the genus provides life-size illustrations with valuable descriptions of habitats and geography. Fowlie trained as a physician, not as a botanist, so his concepts of classification can become idiosyncratic. I often fail to understand why he accepts certain species and rejects others.

*Schultes, R. E., and A. S. Pease. *Generic Names of Orchids: Their Origin and Meaning.* New York: Academic Press, 1963. Why doesn't someone revise, expand, and then reprint this little gem? It may be the most informative yet entertaining example of a plant dictionary in the English language.

*Williams, N. H. "The Biology of Orchids and Euglossine Bees." In *Orchid Biology: Reviews and Perspectives, II,* edited by J. Arditti, pp. 119–171. Ithaca: Cornell University Press, 1982. Reviews the bewildering literature and presents a much-needed table linking bee to orchid species. Let's hope Williams has enough time and tools to test his theories regarding one of the most provocative aspects of tropical evolution.

CHAPTER 11: STEEL MAGNOLIAS?

Coats, A. M. *Garden Shrubs and Their Histories.* London: Longacre, 1963. Alice Coats has had many imitators but no one was ever so adept at spinning together the history of man and his garden plants. Her entertaining style hides her scholarly approach to horticultural books and journals spanning three centuries.

*Dilcher, D. L., and P. R. Crane. "*Archeanthus:* An Early Angiosperm from the Cenomanian of the Western Interior of North America." *Annals of The Missouri Botanical Garden* 71 (1984): pp. 351–383. Fossil flowers are rare because their organs are soft and thin and the flower falls to bits when it dies. Here is how two scientists treated some rare material and how they compared it to the flowers of living plants.

Niklas, K. J. "Turning Over an Old Leaf." *Nature* 344 (1990): pp. 587–588. A popular account of how seventeen-million-year-old leaves made a vast contribution to the new science of molecular paleobotany. If you like Niklas's version, you might want to try to read the scientific paper on pages 656–658 in the same issue of *Nature*. I find the technical account by Edward Golenberg and his six colleagues overwhelming.

*Thien, L. B., W. H. Heimermann, and R. T. Holman. "Floral Odors and Quantitative Taxonomy of *Magnolia* and *Liriodendron*." *Taxon* 24 (1975): pp. 557–568. A novel method was employed to "capture and dissect" floral scents. Ironically, techniques described in this paper are quite dated after less than twenty years. If the study were repeated today, it's likely more fragrance compounds would be discovered in the same magnolias.

CHAPTER 12: COLUMBINES, CUCKOLDS, AND NATIONAL CONTROVERSY

*Grant, Verne. "Isolation Between *Aquilegia formosa* and *A. pubescens:* A Reply and Reconsideration." *Evolution* 30 (1976): pp. 625–628. Grant answers his critics, and the reader is given the unique opportunity to examine a scientist's field notes. The beauty of this paper is that it reviews interlocking publications on the columbines of western America dating back to 1952.

*Segal, Sam. *Flowers and Nature: Netherlandish Flower Painting of Four Centuries*. Amstelveen: Hijnk International, 1990. This book is actually a catalog for an exhibition that toured the world. The stunning and sumptuous accomplishments of Dutch painters over four hundred years are carefully explained. Flower painters range from Jan Brueghel the Elder to Piet Mondrian. See how many times you can spot the columbines.

CHAPTER 13: THE LIFE AND TIMES OF DAFFY-DOWN-DILLY

Blanchard, J. W. *Narcissus: A Guide to Wild Daffodils*. Rugby, England: Alpine Garden Society, 1990. Offers the history of the collection of each species, while clearing up the worst taxonomic tangles. The simple maps make it easy to pinpoint African daffs flowering around Algiers, Tangier, Marrakech, and even Casablanca.

*Brandham, P. E., and P. R. Kirton. "The Chromosomes of Species, Hybrids and Cultivars of *Narcissus* 1. (Amaryllidaceae)." *Kew Bulletin*

42 (1987): pp. 65–102. An exhaustive study featuring photomicrographs of the chromosomes of wild *Narcissus* species, their natural hybrids, and more than two hundred varieties. The text discusses the genealogy of those crosses resulting in such bizarre numbers and arrangements.

*Dahlgren, R. M. T., H. T. Clifford, and P. F. Yeo. *The Families of Monocotyledons.* Berlin: Springer-Verlag, 1985. Why should we care if taxonomists place daffodils and true lilies *(Lilium)* in different families? This is now the most comprehensive treatment to compare and interpret evolution in those plants having only one "baby" leaf (cotyledon) attached to each seed's embryo. The revision concerns all of us who eat corn on the cob and then have pineapple for dessert, drink tequila, spice dishes with ginger or saffron, force hyacinths, rub aloe lotion on our skin, complain about the cost of an orchid corsage, and sit on bamboo furniture.

*Rees, A. R. *The Growth of Bulbs.* London and New York: Academic Press, 1972. Gardeners often complain that botanists do not work for their benefit ("Why are those scientists always changing the names?"). Here is an example of how experiments on the anatomy and physiology of storage organs influences an international industry.

CHAPTER 14: ORCHIDS IN A CEMETERY

*Dafni, A. and P. Bernhardt. "Pollination of Terrestrial Orchids of Southern Australia and the Mediterranean Region: Systematic, Ecological and Evolutionary Implications," edited by M. K. Hecht, Bruce Wallace, and Ross J. Macintyre. *Evolutionary Biology*, Volume 24, pp. 193–252. New York: Plenum, 1990. Dr. Dafni and I decided we'd compare two very different and isolated groups of ground orchids that grow under similar dry conditions. The review will steer the reader toward most of the literature on the pollination of Australian orchids from 1875 to 1986. The most interesting papers tend to be in the most obscure journals and magazines.

Jones, D. L. *Native Orchids of Australia.* New South Wales: Reed Books, 1988. You will not find a more modern or complete treatment of the orchid family in Australia within 656 pages. Every known species has received its own description. The drawings are not the best, but the color photography on almost every page is stunning and leaves nothing to the imagination.

Index

About the Author

PETER BERNHARDT is a professor of botany at St. Louis University and a research associate of the Missouri Botanical Garden. Over the past seventeen years his fieldwork on plant life has taken him across three continents. He has searched for orchids in El Salvador and Chile, caught bees on the wildflowers of tall grass prairies of Kansas, and collected scents from Australian acacias. From 1990 to 1992 he was a curator and writer in residence at the Royal Botanic Garden in Sydney where he examined the reproduction of the golden guine flowers, blue flax lily, sea hearse tree, and the geebung bushes. Dr. Bernhardt and his wife Linda recently purchased their first home and are attempting to restore an old limestone garden.